MARTIN ÓG
MORRISSEY
KINGS FOR ONE DAY

AN AUTOBIOGRAPHY
WITH DERMOT KEYES

HEROBOOKS

PUBLISHED BY HERO BOOKS
1 WOODVILLE GREEN
LUCAN
CO. DUBLIN
IRELAND

Hero Books is an imprint of Umbrella Publishing
First Published 2022
Copyright © Martin Óg Morrissey and Dermot Keyes
All rights reserved

ISBN 9781910827253

Cover design and formatting: jessica@viitaladesign.com
Photographs: The Morrissey family collection

DEDICATION

To my wife Brigid

« CONTENTS »

« ACKNOWLEDGEMENTS »

FOR A MAN who'd talk about hurling morning, noon and night, I probably took my time getting around to put my memories about my life in hurling into print.

But thanks to Liam Hayes and Hero Books, who approached me about working on a book and to Dermot Keyes, who spent a good few evenings in my front room over a cup of tea and a good fire, we've got the job done. I think it's a story worth telling and I'm glad we're after getting what's now here between two covers.

A big thanks to everyone who took the time to talk to Dermot about what I'm often told is one of my favourite specialised subjects… myself! Special thanks to my fellow clubman and Waterford teammate Larry Guinan for sparing the time. We've been friends for life, as indeed I have been with all the men who climbed the steps of the Hogan Stand on October 4, 1959 when we won the Liam MacCarthy Cup. Those from that group who have gone before me are never far from my thoughts.

My family thought a book would be a good idea for me to get involved in and they weren't wrong. It's been great to look back over the span of my life and recall the many good people I met through school, work, hurling and family.

My family is the best team I've ever been part of and I know how good my wife Brigid and my children Eamon, Frank, Martin, Róisín and Niamh have always been to me. Helen, whom we lost at such a tender age, remains the light of our lives.

God bless you all.

I hurled alongside and against some of the greatest men that ever picked up a hurley and I was fortunate enough to play on the most successful teams

Waterford and Mount Sion ever produced.

We had many great days and nights together, and I'm very grateful for each and every one of them. This book has been a great way for me to both remember and honour them.

Martin Óg Morrissey
August 2022

◆◆◆◆◆

TO MAKE THE acquaintance of the great Martin Óg Morrissey in the course of working on this book was an incredible honour for me as both a journalist and a son of Waterford. His is a story I did not expect to piece together. But here I happily am!

This book has brought me into a world that my late father Johnny often spoke of with wide-eyed reverence: the greatest hurling team that ever won 'just' the one All-Ireland Senior Championship. The giants of '59. That gleaming white kit with just a hint of blue. Heroes forever. To shed just a glimmer of light on their brilliance represents the highlight of my career.

To my mother Therese; siblings Gavin, Cathy, John, Kevin and Lillian, and my siblings-in-law Ross, Olivia, Edel and Sandra, who have all endured evenings listening to me rabbit on about any number of topics, often bewilderingly, thanks for staying the course. My late brother Shane, whose second name I proudly share, will forever be honoured by us.

To my partner Avril, who has proven such a wonderful sounding board while I've clanked away on my laptop long into many a night both on this project and many others, a simple thank you is nowhere near sufficient. For this, and so much more, my heart is gratefully oversubscribed.

To my wonderful daughter Bronwyn, whose love of writing and reading has come as such a joy to me, I will offer this advice… keep writing, keep reading and keep smiling.

All my love, Bron. You're one in a million.

I know that my dad and grandparents would have been thrilled to see me work on a book like this. To Johnny, Terry and Lily O'Hara, and Jimmy and Kit

Keyes, thank you all for helping light the fire that's still burning brightly. As long as there's air in my lungs, I'll always do my best for all of you. And to Johnny O'Connor, thanks for that first by-line in *The Munster Express* in the Spring of 1999 and all the faith you've shown in me ever since.

To my many colleagues at the GAA end of my trade, in particular Tomás McCarthy, Phil Fanning, MacDara McDonncha, Brian Flannery, Ger Lawton, Kieran O'Connor, Jamie O'Keeffe, Eddie Kirwan, Tony Ryan, Oisín Langan, Gavin Whelan and Thomas Keane, thanks for all the help. As for the late Kevin Casey, John A Murphy, Tony Mansfield, Seamus Grant and Seamus O'Brien, it was a pleasure to know them all.

To Liam Hayes, part of a Meath team that I idolised as a primary schooler, and whose work had me reading *The Title* every Sunday throughout my mid-teens, thanks so much for picking up the phone for a chat about fleshing out this idea. It's been a pleasure.

To Brigid Morrissey, Frank Morrissey, Bridie Barron, Larry Guinan, Christy Heffernan, Jim Greene, Kevin Fennelly and Phil Fanning, many thanks for making the time to reminisce about Martin Óg and what he means to you.

And to Eoin Fanning, thanks so much for trusting me with an incredible pair of GAA scrapbooks which may well be unrivalled anywhere on the island. To Róisín (who arranged several interviews for me throughout the project), Niamh, Frank, Eamon and Martin, it's been a pleasure to get to know your parents and to be made feel so welcome in your family home, a place full of good humour.

And to Martin Óg, a hundred thousand thanks. It's been quite the journey to get here, over many cups of tea, slices of tart and good humour provided by yourself, Brigid and your family – but we got there in the end!

Dermot Keyes
August 2022

« PROLOGUE »

Martin Óg Morrissey was a hurler too in the true sense. He had his ups and downs, but when he really struck form he could be great and his courage was never doubted. He had the distinction of leading Mount Sion to victory in the Dr Harty Cup in 1953 when they beat St Flannan's, Ennis, the previous year's winners, in the final.

– Raymond Smith, *The Hurling Immortals* (1969)

December 3, 2021
Kingsmeadow, Waterford

THE LUNCH is up. Brigid, my wife of 64 years, has a tray of sandwiches made and the tea is drawing. I've just spent three-quarters of an hour talking hurling. I could have gone on a lot longer – ask anyone I've met over the past 70 years or more and they'll say as much – but it's the middle of the day and the tank needs fuelling.

However, it's not as if the hurling talk came to a halt once the tea was poured.

Holding court at the kitchen table is, a bit like Walsh Park… well beaten ground for me. I've loved the game my whole life. Nearly 89 years in, and despite the modern improvements and innovations in the game that I'm no big admirer of, I'm still very much in its grip.

Brigid pops away from the table to retrieve a memento from my living room. She has her own living room too; it's an arrangement that's served the two of us well, our own Dáil and Seanad. She's only gone a few seconds when she returns to the table with a sliotar, still perfectly stitched 62 years on from the Sunday afternoon it landed in my palm.

I was the last man to touch the ball in play when Jeremiah Fitzgerald of Limerick blew the final whistle to end the 1959 All-Ireland senior final replay.

Waterford 3-12 Kilkenny 1-10.

We'd seen off my parents' people for the first time in an All-Ireland. I'm genuinely amazed we've not repeated the feat since… we've definitely had the raw material since my time, but we're still waiting. The few of us left from '59 really have dined long enough off that win, great and all as it is to be remembered.

To think that Ken McGrath, Tony Browne and Paul Flynn never walked up the steps of the Hogan Stand is hard to believe… we've definitely left at least two All-Irelands behind us since 1998. We've had so many great players over the years, even in those seasons where we couldn't buy a win in the league or championship.

But 60-plus years later, we're still waiting to see the MacCarthy Cup coming back over Rice Bridge. I still hope I'll live long enough to see that thirst taken off us.

THE SLIOTAR IS in my palm again here at home as we have the lunch, while I still manage to get a bit of hurling chat in.

'All Ireland 4th Oct 1959'.

A game and date written onto the ball so as not to confuse it with any of the others I've held onto… and there's a few of them knocking around the house all the while. Now there were a few offers put to us to part with the ball, and sizeable sums were offered too… a year's salary of mine at one stage.

But it's stayed here.

It won't be going anywhere either. There are some things you can't put a financial value on and that sliotar is certainly one of them.

When I remember the great men on both teams who grappled for it that Sunday in October… and to think that I was the one who ended up with it.

It's been a charmed life, alright.

The kitchen table.

Family.

Hurling.

Sure it'd be a much smaller world without the whole lot of them.

The co-author's first encounter with Óg...

MARTIN ÓG MORRISSEY and I first met in his home a fortnight before Waterford took on Galway in the 2017 All-Ireland senior hurling final. It was a genuine thrill for me.

My meetings with the men of '59 have been, regrettably, few and far between. I'd spoken to Frankie Walsh over the phone as a greenhorn reporter during my first working summer back in 2002, and would later meet him socially at an exhibition honouring feted Waterford photographer Annie Brophy.

Frankie, the first captain to climb the steps of the then new Hogan Stand to receive the Liam MacCarthy Cup, was as warm and charming in direct company as he had proven over the phone. I only wish I'd spoken to him more than I did prior to his death in the flickering embers of 2012.

FIVE YEARS LATER, I found myself in the house named 'Banna' for my first sit-down, face-to-face interview with a genuine giant from Waterford's golden era. He may well be the most confident man who has ever hurled for the county. Such confidence might be considered somewhat off-putting from an interviewer's perspective but in Óg's case, it was the opposite.

I was utterly enthralled.

Eighty-three years of age and as sharp as a tack, Óg held court in a manner I became happily familiar with just over four years later as we collaborated on what's between these two covers.

'Ringy? He'd have taken any backline in any generation to the cleaners,' Óg reminisced in his honours-laden sitting room. Referencing Val Dorgan's seminal work on the great man from Cloyne brought the greatest of all time into conversation.

Eddie Keher and John Doyle had already been referenced by my host by the time the chat drifted towards the man who has been joined by Henry Shefflin in the 'greatest ever' debate. *Who's better?*

Who cares.

Can't we just celebrate them both?

'Christy was a gentleman and we became good friends after our days hurling were done with. Whenever we'd be at a match, he had the knack of picking me out in a crowd and coming over for a chat; the lads with me would always wonder what made me so special that Ringy would pick me out, but it all goes back to our playing days, when I had to mark him, and let me tell you, that was some job.

'He was a one-off.

'There was nothing he couldn't do with the ball in his hand. He was as strong as he was skilful, and the ultimate challenge for any back.'

Óg recalled one particular face-off with Ring at the old Athletic Grounds in Ballintemple. 'I'd already beaten Christy to one ball, and being the sportsman that he was, he gave me a little tap on the elbow to acknowledge I'd got the better of him on that occasion.

'Later on in the game, the ball came in his direction, he gathered it and he tried flicking it over my head so that he could run onto it and, knowing him, probably score a goal. But I timed my jump well, caught the ball and drove it 80 yards back down the field.

'I'd no sooner cleared the ball when Ringy said to me, "Tis few lads get the better of me once, Óg, but you've done it to me twice now!" With the ball, without the ball, Ringy was the complete hurler... and it's sad he was taken from us at so young an age (58). He was the total package.'

We then moved on to a chat we'd go into in more detail four winters later... that the decorated Déisemen of the 1957-63 era ought to have taken the game's ultimate honour more than once. Martin Óg clearly agreed. 'That's all we won, the one in '59, when we really should have won more than one,' he exhaled.

'Circumstances and moments in games sometimes go for you and against you, but for me, we should have at least won four All-Irelands between 1957 and '63, and a couple of leagues... we only won one of each.'

But there must be some solace to be drawn from the esteem that Waterford team remains held in? And in re-reading these words, the sentence patterns I've since become readily familiar with really came into evidence.

'There's something in that alright. I remember, it was at Frankie Walsh's funeral, the Lord have mercy on him... we were above in Mount Sion and there were a couple of carloads of former Cork players after travelling down for it, and one of them came over to me and said that the best hurling he ever saw was the type of hurling we played between 1957 and '63.

'He said it was fantastic hurling. And sure Babs Keating said he played hurling, after looking at the way we played, and he decided that that was the way he wanted to play his hurling.'

THE MORNING AFTER the 1959 All-Ireland final replay victory, Martin Óg recalled himself and a few players bandaging up their comrade Larry Guinan, in the wake of some 'tired and emotional' celebrations in Portmarnock.

'Jack Furlong, Lord have mercy on him, he had a bag full of bandages and stuff for rubs and what have you. We got a bandage off Jack, some ketchup down in the (hotel) kitchen and when Guinan passed out that night, we put the ketchup on him and then bandaged him up.

'And when he woke up in the morning, he started asking what was after happening to him and by God, did we laugh. We weren't above the bit of fun ourselves then! We enjoyed ourselves… sure that's what you did after you put in the effort and we had a great time going around the county with the cup after that. We were on the road for about three weeks and it was great. Great memories altogether.'

When asked to describe his team's style of play, Óg spoke with the confidence of Laurence Olivier delivering Hamlet's soliloquy.

'It was fast, open hurling.

'There was no dilly dallying or anything like that. The ball did the work, whereas the way it is now, at the present moment, the men are doing the work. But in saying that, I reckon the biggest team I ever saw playing was the Waterford team that won the All-Ireland in '48.

'There were at least 13 of them six foot and over, and the smallest fella on that team would have been Andy Fleming, who played with Mount Sion. Sure you had Mick Hickey from Portlaw (I can still see Mick striding down the lane off the 'High Road' between Portlaw and Kilmeaden to greet his grandchildren, contemporaries of mine, off our school bus), Christy Moylan, John Keane, Eddie Carew, Kevin O'Connor, Tom Curran from Dungarvan, (John) Cusack from Clonea, Mick Hayes… sure he was well over six foot tall.

'They were big men, and they were great hurlers, and they'd the Celtic Cross to prove it.'

The slings and arrows of outrageous fortune could well have delivered three or indeed four All-Ireland crowns for a Waterford team whose 1959 ascent of Everest has yet to be repeated. But of all the outstanding sides that have won Liam MacCarthy down through the decades, there was surely no other team as good as the side Óg played on which won it just the once.

To share the story of Martin's life in hurling, and his membership of that celebrated team is the greatest privilege of my writing career. I hope you enjoy what we've assembled.

Déise Abú. Martin Óg go deo.

Dermot Keyes
August, 2022

Martin Óg Morrissey back at the scene of Waterford's last All-Ireland Senior Championship title in 1959 when Kilkenny were defeated after a replay.

« CHAPTER 1 »

Early Days in the 'Top of the Town'

Can a first-class soprano or baritone be made? I think not, but a good voice can be made better. If a young fellow has the basics he can be developed into a good hurler, but unless he has the innate fluidity and co-ordination of movement to become a hurling artist, he can never be made one.

— Jack Lynch (interviewed by Raymond Smith, 1969)

MY FIRST MEMORY of hurling was from above in The Sportsfield as it was called then… Walsh Park as it is today. I was about seven or eight years old at the time. My father Ned used to bring myself and my brother Mattie, Lord of Mercy on the two of them, up there. There was a wooden railing down along where the stand is now and we used to sit by the sideline in front of it, watching the matches.

One of the first matches I remember was Mount Sion playing Erin's Own and Nicky Vardy, the Lord of Mercy on him, was playing with Erin's Own and he came out to take a sideline cut right in front of where we were sitting.

Well, he only barely skipped the top of the ball, after which he said, for all of us to hear, 'F**k that ball'. I thought the heavens would open on account of that kind of terrible language… but sure it was nothing in terms of what was said afterwards.

I WAS BORN and reared on Mount Sion Avenue, in a part of Waterford City known locally as the 'Top of the Town', stretching into Ballybricken and along the Yellow Road.

At the top of the street, there were two gable ends of houses – the Barrys and the Collins's – and any day after school, myself and my brother Mattie, two years my senior, could spend three-quarters of an hour or an hour between those gable ends with a hurley and a tennis ball, flicking it here, there and everywhere.

Every fine day, we used to have matches in the street as well. The goal was between an ESB pole and the house, which was only three to four feet across and we had a great rapport with the people in the street… none of them ever minded us playing, except one family, but I won't get into naming or anything like that.

If we happened to break a window, we'd chip in with a penny each to go down and get a pane of glass and a bit of putty, and stick it in… they were quite satisfied with that. There weren't too many windows broken, in all fairness.

The one woman who thought we were bold little boys with our hurleys used to send out her husband… at least that's how it looked to us, and he'd follow us around a bit to try and hunt us away. Now there was one day when both the husband and wife were gone down the town when the breadman, a man called Charlie Henderson from O'Brien's Bakery with his horse and cart, left two buns on one of their window ledges.

When Charlie moved on, we went back up to our house, got a breadknife… then came back down, took the two buns and we went down over a wall at the end of the street. There was a cobbler called Johnson living down behind that wall and he had pigs.

We cut the top slice off the bread, tore the inside of the bread out and filled it up with pig shit. Then we put the top slice back on the bread and left it back on the window sill.

Well, the husband was never sent out to follow us around the street after that!

◄◄◆►►

Bridie Barron (nee Morrissey)

I'M THREE YEARS and seven months older than Martin, so being a bit older than himself and Mattie, I was the sister who ended up looking after the two of them a lot when we were all growing up.

'I was forever running around after them. And I've a memory like an elephant. 'Up the roads' was great. Wherever you looked, you had lovely neighbours… but that's all gone now. We knew every single person on Mount Sion Avenue, Monastery Street, down around Barrack Street… Morrison's Road.

'In the summertime, people sat out on their front steps around here and chatted. It was gorgeous… a lovely way of life. There were so many lovely families around here when we grew up. The Barrons are one of the families that spring to mind. The key was always in the door… you just turned the key and walked in, that's how things were at the time. You couldn't leave your key in the door nowadays.

'As for Martin, he was a right lazy fella, whereas Mattie never sat down… He was hyper. He hurled morning, noon and night, and when he wasn't hurling, he was playing football or handball. Martin was always that bit more relaxed until he really got into hurling and then, there was no stopping him.'

◄◄◆►►

DESPITE BEING TWO years younger than Mattie, I was able to get my game on the same juvenile league team that he'd be playing on. In that league, there was Mattie, Jimmy Grimes and James Grant, who were all the one age… and I always held my own with them, which was great when you were that bit younger. The same thing applied with the street leagues in school when I played with them too. Mattie never minded either… he was a big fan of mine!

He was a good hurler but he was smaller than me, which probably didn't help him. He had two years at minor for Waterford and after we left Mount Sion for a couple of years, Mattie played for Gaedheal Óg, a junior team that was in it at the time, made up of chaps from Mount Sion who hadn't made the cut on the senior team but wanted to keep up the hurling.

They were sporty fellas… they'd head off to Clonmel and Dungarvan for challenge matches and have a day out on the back of them. They wanted to keep playing the game, which was great.

I remember us cycling to New Ross to see Kilkenny play Wexford. My father and my mother Bridie were both from Tullogher in south Kilkenny, about six miles from Ross… and up to the age of 14, I used to shout for Kilkenny. All the big matches we were brought to, including my sisters Bridie and Maura, were the ones Kilkenny were playing in.

I used to spend my holidays at my aunt's above in Ballyhale and whenever we spoke about hurling when we were very young, we were always talking about Kilkenny. And at that time, I thought the nicest hurler I ever saw playing was Jimmy Langton. He was a complete hurler, a top-class wing-half forward.

I really idolised Kilkenny… it was only at 14 that I got sense.

THE LAST DAY I shouted for Kilkenny was up in Dungarvan. The Mount Sion school team was after playing a match prior to a Kilkenny-Waterford match, but that was the last day I backed the black and amber. A few of my team mates did their best to talk some sense into me! My involvement with the Mount Sion club deepened soon after that and my allegiance changed then.

By the way, the sisters were still going to all the big matches up until the Covid outbreak. Bridie was 91 by then and I used to be getting on to her to stay at home and look at the match on television or listen to it on the wireless, not be doing all that travelling… for all the good that did!

◄ ◄ ◆ ► ►

Bridie Barron

'OUT OUR BACK on Mount Sion Avenue, there was a passageway before you went into the gardens. There was a Mrs Moloney living near us and she came out in her yard one day and she looked up, and there was Martin climbing up the chute to get a pigeon.

Sure, the poor woman got a weakness looking up at him… she needed a brandy to settle her nerves and Stephen Greene, who was living next door, had to come out with a ladder to get Martin down.

Another time, my mother was bringing us for a walk down by Reginald's Tower when Martin locked his eyes on another pigeon. He wanted to climb up the tower after the pigeon… he was mad into them, and was for years. After the 1957 Munster final, Martin told me that 10 minutes into the second-half, someone nearby let out pigeons and he was able to tell me the colour of them. I said back to him, "Well, God blast you anyway. There's me sitting on the sideline and I peppering, feeling like I'd a heart attack coming and there's you seeing all those pigeons flying over you out on the field playing at the time!"

'Martin was like a man with eyes in the back of his head out on the field… he had remarkable sight.

'We loved our holidays in south Kilkenny and they certainly left their mark… my grandfather Matt Morrissey was a founding member of the Tullogher GAA club. He lived in Ballymartin in Tullogher and my mother's family came from Glenpike, but there's no-one in that family left now.

One of my mother's sisters was married to a cousin of Jim Kelly, who scored the winning point for Kilkenny in the 1939 'Thunder and Lightning Final' against Cork. She lived in Castlebanny in the parish of Ballyhale and we loved going up to her because she'd let us do what we liked. Oh my God, the freedom… it was great.

'The best times in our lives we spent up there…. the people were absolutely lovely. The front doors were open to us the whole time. I've great memories of that time and I've a great 'smack' for Kilkenny. When Waterford go out of the hurling championship, I'm shouting for Kilkenny.

'I'm a huge TJ Reid fan… the man with the million dollar legs! He's a great hurler and he's like a model as well. I go all the way back to Jim Langton, he was marvellous and then of course you had the Carrickshock crowd, like Jimmy Walsh and Jim Kelly… Jim Kelly was our hero and such a lovely man. Then you had Bill Walsh from Ballough, Peter McBride in Ballyhale… all smashing hurlers.

'My family was hardcore GAA. My father just loved it and an uncle of mine, Phil, was in Croke Park on Bloody Sunday… he was one of the lucky ones that day. He was standing with his back to a wall and he dived to the ground to avoid the gunfire. He never spoke about it, nor did my father.

'I used to try and draw out Brigid's father about his experiences around that time but the most he used to say to me was, "I'm still alive". Republicanism passed down to me from that generation. I went out on the H Block marches.

'It meant a lot to me and it still does.'

◄◄◆►►

GROWING UP, ONLY for hurling, I'd have been lost.

It meant everything to me. To be a top-class hurler, you need to have a hurley in your hand every day… even if it's only for 10 minutes. All those minutes add up.

Hurling was my obsession.

Being good wasn't enough for me… I had to do the best in my position.

I felt that way every time I took to the field and I think that attitude served me well. But unlike Tipperary's Jimmy Doyle, I never brought the hurley and sliotar to bed with me.

The line had to be drawn somewhere!

◄◄◆►►

Bridie Barron

'NEITHER MAURA NOR myself, even though we were mad about hurling growing up… we never had hurleys ourselves. I'd have been terrified to get a belt. I'd have got a weakness thinking about playing camogie when I was of an age that I could have played it, but when I think about it now, at 92 years of age… I'd probably like to have played it.

'And I'd say the reason we didn't even have hurleys then is that we were girls and hurling was for the boys to play. I'm so glad that's changed since then… camogie has come on in leaps and bounds and it's a great game to watch. It's so skilful and Waterford have made great strides in recent years.

'They might end up winning a senior All-Ireland before the men do… we'll see!

'As children, we went to as many hurling matches as we could… the women in our house, my mother included, were as interested in hurling as my father and brothers. I loved hurling from day one. I was lucky enough to be at the All-Ireland final in 1948, the first time Waterford ever won the MacCarthy Cup and the only time we've ever won the minor and senior double… with Mick Flannelly and Jim Ware captaining the teams.

'We grew up with the Flannellys and the Grimeses, the Keanes, Wattie Morrissey, the Powers, John Barron… we all lived in the same part of the city, all within a few streets of each other. It's amazing when you think about it.

'We used to gather up at Mrs Doran's chip shop up on Morrisson's Road and never a bad word between any of them. They were a lovely bunch and a bit of their success rubbed off on Martin when it came to his own playing days, especially in 1959. He was a great presence on the field for Mount Sion, Waterford and Munster and we were always very proud of his achievements as a player and then as a trainer.'

◄ ◄ ◆ ▷ ►

IN THE CITY, we have Mount Sion, Ballygunner, De La Salle, Ferrybank, Roanmore, Erin's Own and St Saviour's all with clubs. De La Salle, Mount Sion and Erin's Own between them used to draw players between Barrack Street and Keane's Road… and that 'square' of streets was where nearly all the hurlers used to come out of.

There were 10 fellas on the Waterford panel in '59 from that big square and they were unlucky not to have a few more. But today, 'down the town' as we used to call it, there's no hurling down there.

Ballytruckle used to have a juvenile team but when they finished at that level, most of them played soccer instead.

Now you could argue that there are more distractions, maybe, in terms of sport in Waterford than in Kilkenny where it's all hurling and camogie… that might well have something to do with it. Now, whether Waterford being a garrison town has anything to do with that is another thing, I suppose.

When you take Ballygunner at the moment, I believe they could put out three teams as far down as under-15. So, when they get past that grade and move onto minor where there'll only have one team, then there's 30 fellas who aren't going to be playing hurling. And a lot of lads, when they don't make it with their own club, sure they just give up playing altogether.

And that's a huge pity, I think.

◄ ◄ ◆ ▷ ►

Bridie Barron

'MARTIN COULD STRIKE the ball on the ground as well as overhead. He was as strong as he was skilful. I could feel my pulse racing whenever the ball came near in… I'd feel like I was running alongside him to chase down an opponent or to collect the ball.

'If he was always a 100 percent out on the field, I was giving it a 100 percent in the stand watching him. I'd come out of the field exhausted.

'Martin would come out in his three-piece suit, not a hair out of place and not a 'morrig' on him!

'God, they were great days.'

The Morrison's Road Street League team, with Martin Óg standing fourth from left. Also pictured (all standing) are James 'Seamus' Grant (first left), John Barron (second from right) and Richie Grant (first on right).

« CHAPTER 2 »

Alone it Stands: The 1953 Harty Cup

GROWING UP, Mount Sion's Paddy Dowling was one of my favourite players. He played left half-back and he could strike a ball from any place… off his toes, off his heel, no matter where it was, and he used to hit the ball close to his body and it's very hard to hook a lad who strikes the ball like that. Paddy was a player that I looked up to from my earliest days going up to the Sportsground.

But we had some great influences off the field too.

When I was going to school, there was a Brother from Belfast called Brother McGill and he was over the under-12 team in Mount Sion. He used to bring us down to Waterpark College and we used to play on their pitch and when he'd go to see a match, he never really went to see the whole match… he'd be going to look at a particular player. He'd pick out all of that player's good points and then write them into his notebook which he brought to every match. He'd be called an analyst nowadays in an inter-county set-up, sat high in a stand, taking notes for a manager.

And then when he was back with us for training, he'd be trying to instil that one particular player's good qualities in us. He really was a fantastic trainer. Brother Carbery had us for the Street Leagues – Morrison's Road – and while we could never win that league, we were the only team that could beat Griffith Place in that competition… yet they nearly always won it outright.

They had a fantastic pick… they'd an awful lot of young fellas, a lot of good hurlers up that way at the time. These were 15-a-side matches, every Tuesday in Walsh Park and you played six to seven matches in it. They were hugely competitive and great to play in. I remember before a final one year, I went out to Tramore with my father and brother… we cycled out, had a swim and then cycled back in. I wasn't worth a tosser playing that day!

There were some great fellas playing in those leagues… Mick Flannelly, John Barron, myself, Larry Guinan, 'Taylor' O'Brien, Jimmy Byrne, Jackie and Joe Condon, Doc Walsh, Dickie Roche… all Mount Sion lads originally. The Condons hurled minor with Mount Sion. What was wrong there was that we had so many players, that when you came out of the minor ranks, there were a good lot of fellas who couldn't get their place on the senior team and a good lot of them gave up hurling rather than go off and hurl for another club.

But Brother Carbery, he was a small man. 'Bunty' we used to call him… now why he got that nickname, I'm not so sure. At the end of the first Street League, we walked into the school and there was a noticeboard up on the outside wall, behind a pane of glass and Bunty was after posting up a synopsis of the games we played in the Street League and in it he described how we played.

And reading what he had to say, given that I thought so highly of him and the way he thought about hurling, it really gave me a big boost. It was great for my confidence. It's hard to put a value on the power of a kind word on a young fella.

In secondary school, we had Brother O'Brien and Brother Kane. Brother O'Brien was from Wexford and Brother Kane was from Clare, but it was Brother O'Brien who had us mostly and he had us up in the field three times a week… Tuesdays, Wednesdays and Thursdays. I played most Saturdays for the club so we always had plenty of hurling.

Brother O'Brien always played a game, and playing a game is the best training you can get when it comes to hurling. At the time, the school had five teams… under-12, under-16, under-16-and-a-half, under-18, and under-18-and-a-half. You had the Rice Cup, along with the Bishop Coholan Cup and the Bishop Hackett Cup… they were two Waterford competitions. Then you had the Dean Ryan and the Harty Cups played at Munster level, so there was always plenty of hurling.

And if you were good enough, you got to progress to the Munster Colleges team for the inter-provincials. I think I set a record by being on that team for four years.

THE ONE TIME I was disappointed after winning a match with the school was the Harty Cup final in 1953. When the referee blew the whistle, my heart sank and we were after winning by a point. I was enjoying the game so much that I was disappointed when the whistle blew.

I was at Jimmy Doyle's funeral in Thurles in 2015 and I was introduced to a priest from St Patrick's College, and he said to me, 'You played with Mount Sion when ye… I'll rephrase that,' he said. 'When you beat us in the Harty final in '53!'

That tells you in another way, just how much I enjoyed the game that day. It was something to have said that over 60 years later. 1953 was my last year in school and that's the first and only time Mount Sion won the Harty Cup. We were the first Waterford school to ever win that competition and it's something I've always been proud to say… that I was a member of that team. Those were great days. Prior to 1953, locally, we used to have great games against De La Salle and the two schools developed a bit of a rivalry. We brought the best out of each other and I think future Waterford teams benefitted off the back of those head-to-heads.

In the semi-final, there were three of us illegal… myself, Jim Power and Joe Goulding, so we weren't played. We'd actually finished school in 1952… that's the year we did our Leaving. But we went back in '53 and we used to draw the dole – you were allowed to draw the dole that time once you'd sat your Leaving. It was 18 shillings a week.

Well, De La Salle objected to the three of us playing and Brother O'Brien told us that we couldn't play and that was it. With seven or so minutes left to go in the match, one of the De La Salle Brothers called over one of his pupils and said, 'Go down to Mackeys on The Quay and order a meal for the team'. They were winning by six or seven points at that stage.

What he either forgot, or just didn't understand, was that no Mount Sion team is ever finished until the final whistle. The boys knocked in a few goals and we ended up beating them by a point or two.

The following morning, we went into school and Brother O'Brien was there. He told us that the objection to our playing was removed, so he said it was up to ourselves if we wanted to play in the final. Playing in the final meant we'd have to give up the dole in the meantime. I looked at the other two fellas and said, 'I'm giving it up anyway!'

And then Jim and Joe said they'd do the same. Joe played in goal… I think he won a couple of junior international caps playing soccer for Ireland after that. He was a very good goalkeeper. And Jim, who is living down in Wexford now, if memory serves me correctly, his father had a barber's shop up in Ballybricken. Jim actually gave up hurling when he moved to Wexford that same year, in '53.

I don't have a clear memory as to whether I'd made a decision to hurl again for the school after doing the Leaving. My best guess, looking back all those years is that Jim, Joe and myself were probably all approached given that we weren't working and were asked would we like to go back and study for another 12 months. So back we went.

You might even say we were the first professional hurlers in Waterford, maybe even in the whole country! Every match that we won, I got the price of the pictures and 20 Players – a win bonus on top of the dole. Now, the thing was that the three of us going back the way we did after the Leaving to keep hurling wasn't just a Mount Sion thing.

Everyone did it. Now, they mightn't all have been drawing the dole alright, but that was our experience at the time. Thurles were the leading school when it came to bringing back players… they definitely had lads playing who were well over minor age when they were brought back.

WE PLAYED ST FLANNAN'S in the final in Thurles, but that wasn't my first time to hurl there. I'd played minor there three years before that. I was on the Waterford minor team for three years but things didn't pan out too well for us then. *Why so?*

Well, in my opinion, during my time on the minor team, we'd have had 10 or 11 very good players in the starting 15, but those were teams that each had a bit of a tail on them because of who they were. I'll try and explain what I mean by that, so bear with me – I mean a team with a name on them. We'd played Tipperary down in Fermoy and the score that day was… well, I bet you'd never guess what the score was?

1-1 to 1-1. There was a breeze there that day… Jesus! A howling breeze.

And the goal that they got… our goalie stopped the ball going over the bar and, as it came down, the breeze blew it into the back of the net. We played with the breeze in the second-half. 'Tidy' Power was playing centre-back and I was playing left half-back and a fella by the name of Geoff Brett – he was from Morrison's Avenue – he was a club mate of mine and he was playing centrefield. He was told going out that he'd be taking the frees and the '70s' and so on.

So, we got a free near the start of the second-half from the half-back line… Clydey Duggan hit it and it went straight into the back of the net. We got a free then, just coming up towards the end of the match and Geoff walked over to take it and I said, 'Geoff, go away, leave Clydey hit it'.

I didn't care who hit it as long as we were going to score. But Geoff says, 'No, I was told to take it,'… he hit it and put it wide. Tipperary walked the All-Ireland that year. We played the replay in Carrick-on-Suir. The first day in Fermoy, Tipperary had two players playing from the year before. The second day in Carrick, they had 10 of them playing, which goes to show they weren't averse to putting out illegal players.

Coming after that, then, there was a bit of a lull. Then in 1954, I got my place in the Mount Sion club's senior team… that was the second year of what would end up being nine Senior Championships in-a-row. In 1962, Larry Guinan was the captain of the team and we played Erin's Own in the county final above in Walsh Park… and I fell on the ground.

One of the Erin's Own fellas, when he passed me, hit me a flog of his hurley. Well if he did, I hopped up, ran after him and hit him a flog of my hurley… we were leading by seven points at that stage and I was sent off.

We lost the game over it.

And it wasn't that I was playing great the same day. I was holding my own, but I wasn't outstanding or anything like that.

Tony Browne, who was 'Fad' Browne's son and had played with Waterford, had a public house in Barrack Street and Tony was playing with Erin's Own that day. He'd played with Mount Sion as a minor, then he went away and came back. After some match that Erin's Own were after playing, he was talking to his father in the bar about going back to Mount Sion, when his father said to him, 'How many Mount Sion men do you see in here?'

'None!' said Tony.

'Well, will you play for one year with Erin's Own?' said his father.

'I will!' said Tony.

Tony won a county senior medal that year. It's fair to say that things worked out well for Tony. He wasn't the last useful stickman out of Mount Sion who'd go by that name.

I THINK THE Mount Sion supporters were more excited than the players were during that successful Harty Cup run. From a player's point of view, all along that run and even in the build-up to the final, things were fairly low key. We did our training three days a week and just got on with it.

We had five selectors on the team… Brother O'Brien, myself – I was also the captain – Paddy Teehan, Joe Goulding and Jim Power, I think, and we sat down and picked the team the same as any other group of selectors would have then and probably still do now. The team, I feel, was always picked fairly. I never felt that there was any favouritism at work.

That didn't really sow a seed for me though, in terms of becoming a selector with the club during the 70s. I trained teams all the way up with Mount Sion… under-14, under-16, under-21 and senior, and we won county titles with all those teams.

Across the river in Glenmore, the teams I trained won junior, intermediate and senior titles and then, training Ballyhale Shamrocks after that, we won a senior championship as well. There's no better habit in sport than winning, and I was lucky enough to end up training several excellent teams that could go toe-to-toe with anyone in the grades they competed in.

Fellas with good attitudes… you can never have enough players like that on a hurling field. If the will to win isn't in the most naturally gifted player, you'll never win anything without a good attitude. That is essential. And I knew after two or three matches if any team I was involved in was going to win anything or not. Talent on its own is never enough in any sport. All the great teams have had a great work ethic. The Waterford team I played in, all the teams Brian Cody has put together in Kilkenny, the current Limerick team and so on… for all the quality in those teams, they'd never have got across the line without the right attitude. They'd have been at nothing without a willingness to work their socks off for the hour or the 70 minutes.

BUT THAT HARTY Cup medal is my prize possession, something which might surprise people who don't know me too well. I think more about winning that trophy that anything else I won afterwards, even the All-Ireland with Waterford in '59.

I was friends with every one of the fellas I was playing with… the whole lot of them. We'd been in school together for 12 or 13 years at that stage and training two or three times a week with the same fellas over all that time. The modern player often talks about all the sessions they do today to achieve success. But to win the Harty Cup for the one and only time in Mount Sion's history probably took all those sessions from when we were very young… beginning at a time when we didn't really know what the Harty Cup even was.

So, to win that cup probably accounted for between 800 and 1,300 training sessions, not that any of us would ever have thought about it that way back then.

We beat Flannan's in that final by a point… 3-2 to 1-7, but that final score doesn't nearly tell the full story. We were well ahead at half-time and then they started picking off points during the second-half but, thankfully, they didn't pick off enough of them. I remember when we sat down to pick the team, Brother O'Brien looked at me and said, 'What do you think?'

There was a chap playing centrefield for Flannan's and, his name escapes me now, but he was from Limerick and he was very useful. Brother O'Brien had brought myself and the other three selectors up to the semi-final Flannan's were playing and afterwards he asked me if he thought we'd win it?

'We will, if we play close attention to the lad in the middle of the field,' I said. 'We'll need to be hard on him.'

'Now we won't be having any of that!' Brother O'Brien replied.

So I had to explain, 'I don't mean to go in dirty on him… we'll have to clout him within the rules, with bodies and keep tabs on him. We'll have to let him know that we're there.'

The match was only after starting when he put the ball on the hurley and came around 'Mogie' Foley and I ran straight into him. I must have shook every bone in his body… because it shook every bone in mine! I stuck him in the ground and for 40 minutes, the chap didn't do a thing. After 40 minutes, he took off with the ball again just like he did in the first minute and I did the same thing I did in the first minute… and completely took him out of the game for the remaining 20 minutes.

I reckon that was the winning of the match that day. Had he been allowed to play up to scratch, he would have been too powerful for us.

I'd a job to do, and I think I did it well.

When the full-time whistle went, the significance of the win didn't fully register. It was only when we got back to Waterford, got off the train over in Plunkett Station and marched down the Quay with the cup… that it dawned on most of us.

We'd become the first school in Waterford to ever win the Harty Cup, something no Mount Sion team has done since.

The Munster Express match report dated March 27 captured some of the excitement of that great day in Thurles:

The game ended in a welter of excitement, as both teams fought for the decisive score. St Flannan's, four points down with ten minutes to go, rallied in traditional style to level the scores on the call of time. Lost time was being played when Matt Morrissey sent the ball between the posts from a 21-yards free to give Mount Sion the all-important score for victory.

When the special train carrying the victorious team and over five hundred of their supporters, most of them juveniles, arrived back in Waterford on Sunday night, a big hosting of boys and adults was waiting at the North Railway Station to give them a tumultuous reception. For many minutes, the deafening cheering continued, and then a triumphal parade was marshalled into formation. It was headed by the Mount Sion boys' flageolet band and, as it proceeded along the Quays, through Barronstrand St, Broad St, etc, to Bunker's Hill and Mount Sion, unbounded scenes of enthusiasm were witnessed.

The captain, M Morrissey, carrying the cup on high, was 'chaired' by the youthful enthusiasts along the entire route, and, in every other respect, the parade was made as memorable as the historic occasion merited. On arrival in Barrack Street, where the Mount Sion Schools are situated, Rev Bro Collins, in a brief address, congratulated the team on the victory and the people for their great reception to the boys. To commemorate the team's deserving win, the boys were given a holiday on Monday.

◄◄◆►►

Bridie Barron

'THERE WAS NOTHING on God's green earth that would have got in the way of me going to the Harty Cup final. As for the excitement that day? Oh my

God, I thought I was going to have a heart attack.

'I remember a Mrs Conlon from Sallypark in Ferrybank. She had a beautiful navy suit on her and when the full-time whistle blew, she took her coat off and then she jumped and danced on it… it was so exciting. Flannan's finished the game so strongly with a run of points and it looked like it was going to get away from our lads.

'But then up stepped Martin to take a free right at the end of the game… but I couldn't look. I closed my eyes as tight as I could and said a prayer that he'd put it over the bar… and he did. A huge shout went up from the people around me, so I opened my eyes and there were arms raised high wherever I looked.

'It was actually hard to take it in, a Mount Sion team doing something they'd never done before and haven't done since. And there was my brother out there as captain of the team, scoring the winning point. Sure we were only bursting with pride watching him.

'And home we came on the train, with a big bonfire lit in Carrick-on-Suir to congratulate the team before we were even back inside the county boundary. And when we were coming into Waterford, over on the rock on the other side, there was another huge bonfire. And of course, the next time the Harty Cup came to Waterford in 2007, Martin's grandson Eoin was on the victorious De La Salle team.

'Six generations of our family have played hurling and football.

'It's a wonderful tradition.'

Phil Fanning

'MOUNT SION WINNING the Harty Cup was a huge thing at the time. I remember being at the match and it was some experience, to go up on the special train service from Waterford to Thurles.

'And I'll always remember Óg taking that '70' to win the match. To put a '70' over the bar at that time was a big thing, given how heavy the ball was. Nowadays, you take it as a given that a '70' will go over every time. It was a real pressure shot but, as calm as you like, Óg stuck it over the bar. And he was recognised as an outstanding schools' hurler at the time as he was picked for the Munster Colleges team alongside players from the North Mon in Cork, Thurles CBS and Flannan's.

'Óg was just outstanding at that time… a class hurler in every sense of the word. That was a very special day for all us Mount Sion lads.'

◄ ◄◆►►

BEFORE WE GOT off the train, Brother O'Brien called me over.

'Where are you going with the cup?' he asked.

'I'm going down the Quay... up the cross and up Patrick Street.'

Brother O'Brien told me, 'No. Don't go near De La Salle... Go up Newgate Street.' So I listened to him and off we went on our procession with the cup. A big crowd followed us down the Quay and we disrupted traffic a bit.

When we were coming through Carrick-on-Suir on the train before reaching Waterford, we passed by Carrick CBS, which was just alongside the railway line, and they lit a huge bonfire for us, something we weren't expecting at all. It was some surprise... we couldn't believe it. Of course, the school in Carrick was the second one founded by Edmund Rice after Mount Sion, so I guess that was their way of honouring the connection after we'd won.

Carrick beat us at under-12 level when we were only allowed to play two from secondary level, while they had carte blanche to pick from both primary and secondary. At that age, a year or two makes a terrible big difference.

After walking through town with the cup, we made our way back up to the school. Brother O'Brien came out and he told me I could bring the cup home for the night and then bring it into the school the next morning... and that's where it stayed for the next 12 months. I was actually surprised I got to bring it home . for the night.

But that meant a lot to me. I'm still the only player from my school that ever got to do that. There are more fellas after walking on the moon than have brought the Harty Cup home as a winning Mount Sion captain.

Sure, why wouldn't I still be proud of that?

AT THE PRESENT moment in Mount Sion Secondary School, the hurling isn't there the way it was in my time. It's strong all the time at primary school level, even though it's about 40 years since the last time they won the Rice Cup... and it's a long time since the secondary school team was a major force in colleges' hurling.

You really need someone in authority within a school to look after young fellas and to develop them as individual hurlers and as teammates. Sure, we saw the proof of that in De La Salle when they won it in 2007 and '08... and then you had the combined colleges in West Waterford winning it in 2012 and '13. It takes a huge level of work to get teams up to that level and it's tough on all schools to reach those levels.

Mount Sion only played in two other Harty Cup finals before '53 – in 1930 and '37 – and we've not played in one since. Winning is great, but it isn't easy.

And that's something we all know about in Waterford.

My father and brother were both at the match... my eldest sister Bridie, who is obsessed with hurling to this day, was there as well. We didn't meet directly after the match. Things were a little different back then when it came to things like that.

There was a Christian Brother who had been transferred out of Mount Sion and up to Derry just before the final, and he was listening out for a report on the wireless. He thought we'd lost by a point, and he fainted! Thankfully, he misheard it and later came to!

Brigid, who I'd marry in 1957, wasn't allowed to go to Thurles for the final... her mother and father were very protective of her.

◂◂◆▸▸

Brigid Morrissey (nee O'Connor)

'MY SISTER GOT to go, but I was stuck at home.

But to give Martin his due, when the team came back to Waterford that night, he brought up the cup to show it to me before he showed it to anyone else.'

◂◂◆▸▸

ON THE MONDAY morning after the final, Brother O'Brien had us assembled outside the school gates and he was after putting a big noticeboard up outside the gate. It was packed with information all about the team, what we'd won and all that kind of stuff.

That was a nice touch.

It made us all feel very good about ourselves, because we were after bringing a great deal of pride to the school and the city. A couple of months later, and I was going out properly with Brigid by then, a few of the boys had been onto me, asking about when we were going to get our Harty Cup medals. Four or five of us were coming up Barrack Street and who was coming against us only three or four of the Brothers… Brother O'Brien included. So I went over.

'Excuse me, Brother.'

'What's wrong with you, Óg?' he said.

'The lads want to know when are we getting our medals?'

And what did he say back to me? 'Sure, it's a ring you want to be sorting out now, isn't it?' And we both had a good laugh about that.

Mind you, in the long run, he wasn't wrong.

WE HAD A really good team, no two ways about it.

Paddy Teehan at centre-half-back was a good hurler. 'Deenie' Breen, who played full-back was injured for the final on account of a broken finger. I played centrefield, so we'd a very strong spine but when Deenie got knocked out, Teehan was shifted to full-back and I went to centre-half-back. Barry Ormonde came out of the half-forward line and into centrefield alongside Mogie Foley, and Frankie Foley came in at wing half-forward.

We'd a very strong group. It was a great team to be part of.

Being captain meant I had some extra bit of responsibility but I didn't really feel it as such, even though I was certainly aware of it. The younger fellas on the team definitely looked up to us.

Those really were the good old days.

Even though we'd won the Harty Cup, there wasn't really any big talk of Waterford benefitting or improving at inter-county level, the way there was on the back of the Waterford colleges' doing well 10 or 15 years ago.

Personally, in '53, the allegiance to the black and amber was still standing against me and I really believe that. But that passed soon enough.

The Coholan Cup winning Mount Sion team (circa 1949), which Martin Óg, holding the trophy, captained and (below) the 1953 Harty Cup winning Mount Sion panel, proudly captained by Martin Óg, pictured holding the prize he treasures above all others.

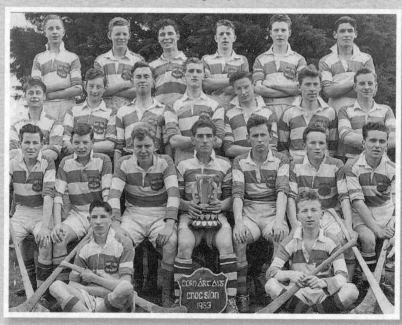

« CHAPTER 3 »

A Natural Born Hurler

IT'S EASY FOR me to talk about the things I felt I did well on the field. That comes naturally. As for any perceived weakness I felt I had, I always found it tough playing on a fast fella. And no matter how good you are, you're always going to meet a man who's better than you… and I had one or two fellas who fell into that bracket. One of them played for De La Salle, and the other with Erin's Own… and it's the Erin's Own lad I remember, Peter McGovern. He was a guard in town.

He was a big, strong man who scooped the ball along with his hurley and I was never heavy enough to knock him out of his stride, so I always found it a challenge to mark him. Now the De La Salle man, whose name eludes me, well he wasn't really a hurler at all… he was the furthest thing from a hurler you could imagine, but I just couldn't handle him. He held the hurley in the unorthodox way – like a right handed golfer would with the left hand on top – and to this day, I still can't fathom what it was like to mark him.

ONE NIGHT YEARS ago, I was talking to Jimmy McGinn, who founded the Ballygunner club when there was barely a dozen houses in the parish, and he said to me, 'When we met Mount Sion, I'd never had any qualms about any of the rest of the players, but I could never get a man in Ballygunner to hurl you. I tried every type of player on you… rough fellas, smooth fellas and so on, so I then decided to put a complete hurler on you, a fella by the name of John Curran!' Now, I went to school with John and he was a lovely hurler, but he was very timid. Jimmy said he watched me for the first quarter of an hour in that particular match and how I watched John moving this way, then that way… and then the next minute, John went for the ball and I hit him.

As Jimmy put it to me, 'And that was the end of John!'

Neither Philly Grimes nor Seamus Power ever worried Jimmy too much, so he told me, but he could never get a Ballygunner man to master me.

I remember another chat I had some time ago with Austin Flynn, the Lord have mercy on him, below in Dungarvan when he received an award from the Western Board, and I got up that night and said a few words about Austin. When he made his own remarks, Austin said, 'That man gone down there now was the best hip-to-hip hurler I ever saw playing'.

First time hurling was very much my strongpoint. I could hit a ball over the bar from 80 yards out off the ground and that was no mean feat at that time. There's a lot of talk nowadays about fellas scoring points from sideline cuts 30 to 40 yards out… I could do that from 50 to 60 yards. In the drawn All-Ireland final in '59, the ball that Seamus Power got for his goal came from a sideline ball that I took well inside my half… and he got the ball in at corner-forward, and stuck it in the back of the net.

It just came naturally to me, which probably explains why I could strike the ball such distances, be it from a sideline cut or open play. Brother McGill, Frankie Walsh and myself were having a chat one time when Frankie asked Brother McGill, 'How do you make a hurler?'

Before the Brother got a chance to reply, I asked if I could answer Frankie's question first and he graciously conceded, saying, 'I'd love to hear your answer.'

'You're born with it,' I simply told them.

Brother McGill looked at me and said, 'You're quite correct'. If you haven't got it, you just haven't got it. The best trainer in the world can't put the touch or the timing into any hurler. He might well be able to hone those qualities in a better way, but if they're not there in the first place, you're going nowhere.

Skill comes naturally. It's as simple as that… it's instinctual. When I was training teams myself, no matter how much training some lads did… and they put the time in to give them their due, it just didn't come for some of them.

And it never did.

A match above in Dungarvan, against the CBS, springs to mind and again I can't think of the name of the chap I was marking, but he was at least two steps faster to the ball than I was… but I still hurled the ears off him. When he got to the ball, he had to stop while I'd be coming in pulling and I clattered the ears off him.

Three months later, we played again in a competition, this time in Walsh Park and in between those matches I'd heard that he'd been training every single day to get his own back on me. Well, in came the first ball between us and… BANG!

The chap had to go off… four fingers broken. From what I could gather, he never again played hurling after that.

IN ALL THE years I played, the day that still stands out for me in terms of how I performed is the Harty Cup final. I know I couldn't have played any better than I did that day. For Waterford, the 1962 Oireachtas final against Tipperary in Croke Park is the one that really comes to mind after all these years. Prior to that match, we were walking up from the hotel to Croke Park and there was a pipe band walking along in front of us. I turned around to whoever was behind me.

'I'm going to play some game today!' I told him. And I did.

I couldn't have got any more out of myself than I did that day. And in the following week's *Waterford News & Star* report (October 23, 1962), 'Deiseach' pretty much said as much:

The last of the defenders was, indeed, the greatest of the great on Sunday. None will dispute the right of Martin Óg Morrissey to be so described. Were I to award a star of the week medal it must go to the man from the Monastery.

He literally blasted Tipperary with a display of hurling not often seen in Croke Park. He met man and ball, and belted both with equal facility. On the ground or in the air, deep in defence or driving the attack, Morrissey was supreme.

Here was a tour de force. For a student of hurling, for the purist who pines for the glories of old, here was a study in hurling perfection.

We were in the dressing room after the match and I was taking down my shirt off the hook, when I got a tap on my shoulder. I turned around and who was standing there only Austin Flynn.

He put out his hand and, honest to God, he said to me, 'Thanks for the medal, Martin!'

'Well, that's okay," I replied. 'You're quite welcome!'

Austin was a great man to put something onto a story. When he got back in Dungarvan, he was telling a fella about what had happened above in Croke Park. 'I tapped Óg on the shoulder and said, "Thanks for the medal"… then I put out my hand and we shook on it.'

As Austin told it, I replied, 'You're welcome… but where are the other 13 handshakes?'

◄ ◄ ◆ ► ►

Phil Fanning

'I'LL NEVER FORGET that Oireachtas final, the day Óg won more than one medal as he's often put it himself down through the years.

'I was sitting in on the sideline in front of the old Cusack Stand and that was a match Waterford weren't expected to win that day, which is worth remembering. Over on the far side of the field from where I was sitting, in the corner between the Canal End and the Hogan Stand, the ball went down that flank and Óg came out for it as Mackey McKenna set off after it.

'Óg got to the ball first and as he turned, McKenna came in on him and he took McKenna on the shoulder and dumped him on the ground. And he'd no sooner done that, when Liam Devnaney came in to try and, to be honest… take Martin Óg out, but Óg stood his ground and Devaney ended up on the ground as Óg whipped the ball down the field about 70 or 80 yards.

'And you have to remember the weight of the sliotar in those days and to think of the distance he could send it. A lot of people talk about the speed of the game now, but if you had the likes of Martin Óg, Frankie Walsh, Philly Grimes and Mick Flannelly hurling then with the ball that's used now – Eddie Keher and Jimmy Doyle too for that matter – the things they would have done.

'There'd have been no comparison given the skills those players had. Óg always did his bit but he was exceptional in that Oireachtas final.'

◄ ◄ ◆ ► ►

THE 1963 LEAGUE final against Tipp was another day when I knew I couldn't have hurled any better than I did, and that's a very satisfying feeling. Players know when they're on full throttle. They don't need anyone to tell them when things are running smoothly. At Jimmy Doyle's funeral in 2015, I met John 'Mackey' McKenna – he was playing centre-forward for Tipperary back at that time – and we were talking away, when a couple of fellas from Cork came over to us and Mackey told them, 'You see that fella there? That was the best centre-half-back I ever played on!'

Now that's saying something, to have that said over 50 years later. Sure that could only fill you with pride.

To win anything in hurling, your half-back line has to be dominant. Just look at Limerick in the last few years and how their line has operated. And it's not all about being the fastest or the strongest either. Take Fergal Hartley, for example and all the years he hurled for Ballygunner and Waterford.

He was neither the strongest nor the fastest player, but there were few better readers of the game than Fergal. The same goes for 'Brick' Walsh. Both of them knew where they needed to be when the ball was coming down their end of the field. And how often did either of them lose the ball once they had it? Rarely, if ever.

Brick was a great centre-back despite not being able to stroke the ball over great distances. And when he went into the forwards, Brick was able to shift the ball onto a better finisher. He was a fantastic man to win the ball, just as Hartley was and we were lucky to have them for all those years.

The really good players will always listen to a trainer, the way I did with Brother McGill in Mount Sion, who is only trying to make them better. For me, you could see that written all over Fergal and Brick and the way they hurled. I can't imagine either of them shied away from good advice.

Anyone who doesn't listen to a trainer or take on board what a more experienced player is willing to pass on during training or a match, they're not going to make it. Young lads think they know it all. By the time I was 40, with my best days on the field well behind me, I knew I was still only learning about the game. All the confidence in the world counts for very little without humility.

WHEN I HURLED, myself and the fellas I played alongside wanted to win as much as the lads playing inter-county do today. The big difference between now and then, though, is there wasn't as much emphasis on winning then as there is now.

You have to win every match now or, as some would have you believe, you're at nothing. It's something that's been imported from other sports over the years and you even see it in the way games are written and analysed about now. For me, I don't think that has done anything for the game.

I don't think it's made today's players better.

In my time, you went out and you played the game and you enjoyed it. If you won, you won and if you lost, *you lost*, whereas now if you lose, you're down in the dumps for the following 12 months… or longer in some cases. I think we enjoyed the games more so than the current generation does.

The modern hurler now has to train night and day, doing sessions at six and seven in the morning and so on. We'd be barely thinking about getting out of bed at that time, never mind being up and ready to train.

If a player gets rid of the ball quickly, he takes himself out of trouble and you won't be getting physically punished. There are too many frees in the game at the present moment. When you look at fellas scoring a goal and 13 points… and they after getting a goal and 11 off frees, there's something wrong there when the likes of that is happening so much of the time. And it's going on for a good number of years now. But if you get the ball in your hand and you run with it and hit a man, you're charging with the ball and the free should be against you, but at the present moment, more often than not, the man charging gets the free.

That makes no sense to me… and if the bigger man has the ball, sure he'll nearly pick out the smaller fella to take him out.

There's a lot of talk about hurling culture nowadays but I think that it's always been there. We just mightn't have always labelled it that way. If you go over to Kilkenny and you go to a juvenile match, the mothers and the fathers of players in a lot of cases will be there, supporting their young lads… but when you go to the same game in Waterford, I don't think it's the same. Now it might be after changing a bit the last few years, but I still think you have a lot more young lads in Waterford heading off to matches with no-one from home going along to shout him on.

I really do think that encouragement matters and keeps lads interested.

You only have to look at the Kilkenny lads going to school with the bag over their shoulder and the hurley in their hand. We've never had anything close to that in Waterford. You look at what Kilkenny have done through different generations and then you look at how close Waterford have come in the past 20-odd years.

You'd have to wonder what's the thing we've missed. Kilkenny and now Limerick... they've got across the finish line and then repeated the trick.

I REMEMBER PLAYING a junior match for Mount Sion out in Ballyduff (Lower). Tommy Morrissey, Lord have mercy on him, was playing left-half-back and I was on the left side of centrefield... I ended that match with eight points from play. And this was all I did... when their fellas were pucking out the ball, I turned and I faced Tommy and he'd go up, bat down the ball to me... then I'd catch it and BANG... I stuck it over the bar. Hurling is a simple game.

And when you play it in a simple way, when you play it the right way, you'll win far more games than you'll lose. A team that fields well, passes well and shoots well is rarely beaten. Nowadays, there's too much handball in hurling... and that goes for football too. If I'd any say in the rules of both codes now, I'd crack down on the amount of handpasses... too many games now are like basketball the way the ball is flung around.

And the handpass itself now in hurling is basically a thrown ball a good deal of the time, and I hate to see the ball being thrown in hurling.

My first instinct, whenever the ball came my way, was that I was going to strike the ball and where I was going to hit it. It was all about putting it somewhere I could hurt the opposition, either into one of our forwards or over the bar. I was never, ever thinking about a five-yard pass going sideways across the field into our centre-back... and I never considered passing the ball back into our full-back or into the corner behind me.

I knew the days when I was going to play really well, but I can't really explain how I knew that. The hairs on the back of my neck would be nearly standing out straight the morning of a match, and on those mornings, I knew I'd dominate the fella I'd be marking that afternoon. And more often than not, the hairs were up on the neck most Sunday mornings.

I could feel it in my bones. Now you might think you'd hit days like that once in a career. Well, I was lucky, since I had quite a few of them!

Training with Waterford in Munster colours (above) and posing with newborn son Eamon (below) with the spoils of 1959 (and with the '53 Harty Cup panel framed on the wall).

« CHAPTER 4 »

The Monastery Man

You have heard of Sean Óg's Rockies, Kilkenny's Tullaroan. You have heard of Limerick's Eire Óg, and Waterford's Erin's Own. They all rank high in rhyme and song, but now I'll give you mine, here life and health, good luck and wealth, to the hurlers of Mount Sion.

– The Mount Sion Anthem (circa 1930)

MY PLAYING DAYS with the Mount Sion club began in earnest when I hurled minor in 1949 and I'd end up winning two minor championships with them. Waterford had won both the senior and minor All-Ireland titles the previous year, so it was a great time for hurling in the county, but I can't say either win made me any more motivated than I already was.

I was 14 years of age at the time and a bit too young to be considered for the county minor team. Mount Sion had five players on the minor team in 1948, with Mick Flannelly the captain, and the great John Keane led the way for the seniors when they beat Dublin in Croke Park, scoring 3-2 out of Waterford's 6-7.

It's a double we've never repeated since.

When I hurled minor with the club, there happened to be three Morrisseys playing on that particular team – and their first names were Martin, Mattie and... yes, Martin.

Martin, from Griffith Place, was two years older than me, so the fellas looking after us started calling me Martin Óg… and all I was ever called after that when we played was Óg. And it has stuck ever since.

It hadn't anything to do with a grandfather or uncle or anything like that as is so often the case in the association. Necessity gave me my nickname. Hurling provided me with my second christening.

NOT TOO LONG after my time at minor level ended, I had a bit of a disagreement with the club and that led me to hurl with the Gaedheal Óg junior team for two to three years, before I rejoined the club in 1953, the second year of Mount Sion's nine in-a-row sequence of Waterford Senior Championship victories.

I left the club over my brother Mattie.

We were playing in Dungarvan and the bus we travelled on for matches at the time used to pick up most of the players on Slievekeale Road, the road which runs directly behind the main stand in Walsh Park. When we got on the bus, there were two fellas missing… one was gone off playing tennis, what the other fella was doing now escapes me.

Anyway, one of the top officials in the club declared there and then that neither of the two men on the missing list would play for us again. Off we went to Dungarvan and we beat the ears off them.

The next match was above in the Sportsfield and myself, Mattie and the rest of the lads were togging off when the team was called out. Lo and behold, the fella who'd played tennis while we were in Dungarvan was named in the team. Mattie looked up and said to the official, 'You said that he'd never again play for Mount Sion'.

The official replied, 'Ah sure, that was only heat of the moment talk!'

Mattie wasn't having it.

'That's it,' he said. 'I'm not playing any more with ye.'

He took off his jersey and walked out the door. I hurled on for the rest of the year with Mount Sion but at the end of the year, I went to Gaedheal Óg, a nice bunch of fellas but not a club with high aspirations… all of them would have hurled minor with Mount Sion. There were a lot of good hurlers among them but collectively they lacked the killer instinct. Blood proved thicker than water.

I felt I had to show loyalty to Mattie at the time. He did what he thought was right and I can't blame him for reacting the way he did. The club official had said one thing and then went back on his word the very next match, and Mattie felt he couldn't stand that sort of hypocrisy.

The club, through Wattie Morrissey – a son of his won an All-Ireland minor medal in 1948 – attempted to change our minds at the end of that year. It took a few years but we did return to the fold… after a good deal of persuasion when it came to Mattie. He told me he was going back, so I went with him.

Now, Mattie only came back for a year or two before returning to Gaedheal Óg, but I stayed put after that. When Gaedheal Óg finished up, Mattie went to Erin's Own, where a lot of lads who couldn't get their place on the Mount Sion senior team ended up playing, including Jimmy Grimes, a brother of Philly's. Mattie and Jimmy were great friends, they were always together.

IT DIDN'T TAKE too long for me to settle back into Mount Sion colours, although it did take me a while to get back into the starting team. Up until then, I'd mostly hurled in centrefield or wing half-forward, but the chap who was playing left-half-back in one particular championship match wasn't up to scratch… and I was playing corner-forward.

We were losing at the time when the men on the line switched the two of us around… I'd a stormer at wing-back and the other fella ended up scoring two goals. It worked out well for the two of us. We were then named in the same positions for the county final and I was delighted to be playing left half-back again. It was my favourite position and it's where I'd end up playing my best hurling for both club and county.

I could read the game really well from that position. Philly Grimes was playing centre-back and I was able to cover behind him when he moved out of position, or the odd time he'd miss a ball… and he didn't miss many, I can tell you. They'd be talking about sweepers today as if it's a new invention. It's anything but!

Between myself on the left and Tom Connolly at right half-back, we swept for Philly when we needed to and we developed a great understanding. There was no great discussion about it either. We played to our strengths and worked a lot of the time off our instincts. We'd a great understanding as a half-back line.

The nine in-a-row team was a brilliant one to play on. Had we had Munster and All-Ireland Club Championships to hurl in at the time, I've no doubt we'd have picked up a few along the way. Seven Mount Sion players started the 1959 All-Ireland final for Waterford, so we were more than good enough to compete at that level.

We had some great battles throughout those years but we found a way to keep on winning. For sure, we had a lot of days when we knew we were going to win but that never took away from the satisfaction of winning senior titles. We kept wanting to improve. And it didn't matter where we played those finals… be it in the Sportsfield or below in Dungarvan.

The Fraher Field surface was generally excellent and I always liked playing there. And they had it drained well until a circus went in on it and broke up some of the drains when they were putting down stakes. It took years after that to get the pitch right again. It's a more open field than Walsh Park, so the breeze was always a bit more of a factor in Dungarvan than it ever was in Waterford.

When Paddy Greene, the Lord have mercy on him, was training us in Mount Sion, every night we played a match… and there was always a bit of aggro. One night up there, Paddy asked myself and Seamus Power to pick a team each, and one of the lads I picked was a big young fella called Michael 'Ux' Frisby from Cannon Street.

Ux and myself played in the centre of the field and I told him we'd give Power a bit of a rattle. Not long after the match started, Power went for a ball… bent down to pick it up and as he did, Ux ran into him and put Power spinning. Then Seamus came towards me and I stuck him into the ground with a shoulder.

Paddy blew the whistle. Power got up off the ground, shook himself, then put the ball down and stood over it.

'What are you doing, Seamus?' Paddy asked him.

'I'm taking a free,' said Seamus.

'Sure the free's against you, boy!' Paddy replied. 'You held the ball too long.'

Things used to be hot and heavy during training, not that it did us any harm.

I WAS CAPTAIN of the team in 1961, and that was a great honour for me.

John Keane had captained the senior team for a dozen years or more and for each of those years, when other players were put forward as an alternative captain, the club hierarchy basically told us that once John was playing, John would be captain.

That wasn't John's doing, but that's how things were. Nonetheless that came as a big disappointment for a lot of other Mount Sion players.

Andy Fleming (1916-2011), a great bit of stuff on the field for club, county and province, played his last ever match when he hurled for Munster in the Railway Cup final in Croke Park on St Patrick's Day in 1951. It came as a huge surprise.

Andy was 35 at the time… he had played his part in the 1948 All-Ireland win and he felt the time was right to bow out. Not many play their very last match in Croke Park, but Andy did. Over the years, I met Andy from time to time and one particular day I asked him why he retired when he still had loads of hurling in him?

'The main reason was I'd never been captain of Mount Sion,' he told me, and he didn't say much more than that. By the time I started playing, the club introduced a new rule in which you could only be senior captain for a year at a time… you could captain the team again down the line alright but not in successive years.

It was a much fairer way of giving players – and we weren't short of good ones, let's face it – an opportunity to captain the team.

I didn't really have a brand of captaincy. It wasn't as if I had to say a specific few words in the dressing-room either before or after a match. It wasn't ever like the way rugby has always been, where the captain is almost part of the management team.

Before most matches, Pat Fanning used to say a few words to gee us up… more so with the county than with the club, but he was about the only official who ever did that regularly. And he was a great man to talk before a match. I remember one day in Dungarvan when Pat gave such a spiff that if we'd been playing the Rest of Ireland that day, we'd have wiped the floor with them.

My main task as captain was to go up for the coin toss… that's how I viewed it. No more than the 'cult of the manager' that's developed over the last 30 years, there's too much made of who is captain. But don't get me wrong, to be captain of Mount Sion on senior final day was a great honour. And to be captain on a team with so many great players… so many good men, that was never lost on me.

The days we won senior finals in Walsh Park, afterwards we'd head to Mikey Norris's pub on Barrack Street with the cup… we didn't have far to travel. The last time it happened with our team was in 1961 when I was captain… and beyond that, winning Mount Sion teams would go down to John Keane's pub, further down Barrack Street.

When we won a final played in Dungarvan, we made for Mickey Landers' pub on the corner of Grattan Square. We always marked the occasion well.

It's easily done with a good bunch.

In 1962, our great run came to an end in the final against Erin's Own following a replay, a game I was sent off in after I hit a fella a clout across the arse with my hurley. He had hit me when I was after falling on the ground.

Well, up I got and ran after him, and I exacted my retribution. However angry I was when I pulled on him, I was 10 times more annoyed with myself afterwards for losing my cool. I was sent off once as a minor player, once as a junior and once as a senior, but we lost to Erin's Own that day because I blew my top.

We'd have won 13 in-a-row if I hadn't lost the run of myself.

All these years later, I'm as disappointed with myself for that as I am with the fact that, somehow, the Waterford team I played on only won that single All-Ireland. There are definitely a few medals missing from the sitting room display all the time. After I took the long walk, Erin's Own struck two more goals and we ended up losing by 5-7 to 1-14, the first time we'd lost a championship match since October 1952.

It was Erin's Own's first title since 1947, and they haven't won the senior championship since.

The *Waterford News & Star's* (November 27) match report attempted to wrap up the previous decade, the greatest in the club's history, in a few well-considered paragraphs.

But what of Mount Sion, the men who had not suffered a championship defeat since October of 1952? How did they fare in defeat? Let it be recorded that they had to give best to a superior combination on the hour's play. But let all recognise the quality of their effort as they made their second half bid to achieve the impossible, to turn the tide, and snatch victory from certain defeat, as they had done so often in the past.

Mount Sion were trailing from the start. They faced the second half with a crippling deficit. They cut that deficit. They kept the issue open and they failed only because of the quality of the opposition, and of the Herculean efforts of an Erin's Own defence which in the climactic last quarter assumed heroic proportions.

Yes, a title was wrested from Mount Sion; a record was denied them. But, in the manner in which they fought by the spirit that enabled them to fight back when others might have despaired lies the proof of a truly great club.

DURING THAT LONG winning run, I don't think we ever considered ourselves invincible or anything like that. We had a bit of luck along the way, like all successful teams do. You don't hit 10 out of 10 every time, and some days it was more about getting the right result than producing fireworks.

One of the years that we beat Erin's Own in the final, Philly Grimes and his father were talking away… now remember, Philly's brother Johnny was hurling for Erin's Own.

'Philly!' his father told him, 'The medal you have today should be around your brother's neck.' And he was right. Erin's Own should have beaten us that day, but they did stop us winning 10 in-a-row, so there must have been a lot of satisfaction for them when it came to halting our gallop.

They gave us some great matches and they had two guards from Carlow on the team – Willie Walsh and Peter McGovern – who'd have got their place on any senior club team at the time.

Abbeyside were formidable opponents at the time. Austin Flynn and Johnny O'Connor were the stand-out names and they never gave you anything easy. We played them in a county final above in Fraher Field and Johnny was playing centre half-back like myself that day.

We were both having a whale of a game as half-time approached but, after the break, Johnny was switched into centre-forward so we were in direct company out on the field.

He didn't hit another ball for the rest of the match. If Abbeyside had left him at centre-back, they'd have put us to the pin of our collar that day.

We were conditioned to win.

That was the Mount Sion way.

So whenever we lost, it came as a huge disappointment. If you lost on a Sunday, you'd still be annoyed about it the following Wednesday. The best way to get over losing a match was to go out and win the next one, and we always measured up well in terms of how we reacted to losing.

Funnily enough, my best playing memory with the club wasn't any of the senior finals. It was in the 1961 Dunhill Tournament final against the Kilkenny champions Bennettsbridge… and it was considered an unofficial All-Ireland Club Championship at the time. We were down by 13 points at half-time and we turned it around in the second-half to win by five or six points. That was very satisfying.

We played them in a tournament in New Ross as well and beat them by a point, with John Flavin scoring the winner. Those were two huge tests of us… we stood up to Bennettsbridge in both of those games.

◄◄◆►►

Phil Fanning

'THE MOUNT SION/BENNETTSBRIDGE matches in Dunhill were marvellous. Mount Sion made the Dunhill Tournament because the teams that came to play in it… Rathnure with the Rackards, St Aidan's with Nick O'Donnell, 'Padge' Kehoe… they came to play Mount Sion. And then of course, you had Glen Rovers who used to travel up from Cork in Austin Princess taxis… bigger than London taxis, in fact they were more like limousines.

'They travelled up for one particular final in the late 50s/early 60s and between 3,000 and 4,000 turned up to watch the match. Nearly everyone there had cycled out from town to go see it… I cycled out to Dunhill umpteen times for matches myself. Across the road from the pitch, which was a plain field at the time with no buildings on it, the Harneys, the local publicans, were running a bar on the evening of the final.

'There were spinners there and all sorts of other attractions, all of which helped to make a real occasion out of the match. There were no dressing-rooms in Dunhill at the time, so the Glen togged out in the local primary school. The game was meant to throw in at 7:30pm and Mount Sion were out in the field ahead of the scheduled time.

'This was midsummer and it was a fine evening, so there was plenty of daylight. So Mount Sion were out on the field, pucking around and there was no sign of the Glen appearing.

'By a quarter past eight, they still hadn't appeared, when word got as far as the pitch that they weren't going to leave the school until they got their expenses paid to them in full… in cash, from the takings at the gate. They weren't leaving the school until they each got it put into their hands.

'Tommy Glasheen, a Tipperary man who ran the tournament at the time, had to go up to the school with the money from the gate and hand it to each of them. The game eventually started at nine o'clock and finished just after 10. I doubt if there was ever a later throw-in time in Dunhill!

'Luckily, it was one of those fine, bright summer evenings. The Glen won the game by about 10 points… that was certainly one of the more famous hurling nights out in Dunhill.

◄◄◆►►

PADDY GREENE – 'GREENER' as he was known to many – was our trainer throughout the nine in-a-row run and beyond that as well. He had his own way of preparing a team and always seemed to know how to put a spark into the 15 fellas taking to the field.

He had a very straightforward philosophy.

'The way you train, is the way you play.'

That certainly worked for us.

We used to have a match every Tuesday and Thursday night in the field among ourselves. We played for an hour, switched ends at half-time and left nothing behind us.

The bit of aggro was there right from the throw-in and I think that's what Paddy was looking to develop in all of us… what's called 'the edge' nowadays. I think we gave him what he wanted, and it's what helped us stand up to everyone during that long unbeaten run in the senior championship. After the match most nights, we'd run laps and do sprints, but there was hardly any specific stickwork during Paddy's sessions.

The match looked after that. We just went out and played.

Paddy treated every one of us the same. It didn't matter to Paddy whether you were inter-county or not. Mount Sion is what he was interested in and that was it. I often wonder if Paddy had been involved with the county team, would we have won more? That he was never involved at inter-county level, when you consider what he achieved with Mount Sion, is hard to credit. He had a great way about him with players and most of the matches he trained us for, we won. His record speaks for itself.

The main reason Paddy was never involved was down to the involvement of John Keane and Pat Fanning with Waterford as selectors. At that time, the inter-county management team had five selectors. For most of the 50s, given the success Mount Sion enjoyed in the senior championship, we had two selectors – John and Pat. Then you had one selector from the losing senior finalists and the remaining two were proposed and seconded at a county board meeting.

Paddy never got an opportunity with Waterford and if it bothered him that he had missed out, well he never let it show. John's reputation spoke for itself… he'll always be one of the greatest figures in the history of both Waterford and Mount Sion, but it was an unfortunate coincidence for Greener that they were both training teams through the same period.

John did serve as a selector with the club and though he never trained us, he never missed a game we played in either. He was a very quietly spoken man and, just like Paddy, he treated everyone the same. They both gave so much to hurling. John was only 58 when he died in 1975. And to think Christy Ring was only a few months older than John when he died four years later. Both taken far too soon.

THE MATCHES THROUGHOUT that period of dominance Mount Sion enjoyed were often tough. We certainly didn't get things easy. We were above in Cappoquin one evening playing Tourin in the Sargent Cup and our six forwards were made mincemeat of that night. What a gruelling they got. Funnily enough, all of our backs, myself included, came out of that match unscathed and intact.

When the final whistle blew, Pat Fanning came out and gestured us up to Cunningham's Hotel, where we got stripped off and dressed for the spin home. 'Don't any of ye walk there on your own,' Pat warned. 'Make sure ye're in twos or threes.'

Well, I'd my eye fixed on Philly Grimes to 'pal up' with for the walk… I knew I'd be safe alongside Philly. So we walked down the road and a fella jumped out in front of us and started making a few shapes. BANG!

Philly stuck him into the ground with a dig… he was deadly with his fists. I'd have stood in front of Philly with my hurley, but I wouldn't have stood in front of him if I was relying on my fists. He'd cut you asunder.

You couldn't have asked for a better teammate than Philly. They didn't come any tougher and he always had your back.

More people went to the club matches in the 50s than they do nowadays.

There used to be lads up on walls and hanging out of trees to watch some of the games. No health and safety in those days. County final day had a great sense of occasion about it.

People's options were a bit more limited at that time, granted, very few people had televisions – the wireless was still king in most houses – and if you wanted to see your team playing, through the turnstile was your only option. But when you're playing, whether it's in front of a few hundred, a few thousand or over 60,000 in Croke Park, I don't remember the size of the crowd making too much of a difference in terms of how I played.

I think how you played on any given day depended on what type of a humour you'd be in, more than the number of people watching you. Now you wouldn't be totally unaware of it the whole time, but the less you heard of that or the less attention you paid to it, the better you hurled.

I've heard a lot about pre-match routines over the years, and I think it's something you'd associate more with soccer than you would with hurling or football… a fella always putting his left sock on before his right and so on, but I never consciously had one of my own before any match I played.

Whatever space was empty in a dressing-room, I took it.

I never had a big level of nerves in the system before a match either. It's funny what other people would pick up on, though. Paddy Greene had his two eyes fixed on me when I came out onto the field before the 1959 Munster final against Cork in Thurles.

'Jesus, there's something different about Óg today,' he said. He saw something he hadn't usually seen in me. I was all tensed up, and I didn't play what I considered my usual game. By the time the National Anthem was played, I knew if I was going to play well or not.

It was just a feeling I had in my body. The hair stood up on the back of my neck and I just got on with it.

The Morrisseys, Brigid and Martin Óg, looking every part the dashing young couple on the street in Waterford

« CHAPTER 5 »

The Last Hurrah with Cnoc Síon

I'D A GREAT run on Mount Sion's senior team, playing from 1953 through to '74, and I went out on a high, winning another senior championship after we beat Portlaw, who were going through their most successful ever period at the time – they won five of their six senior titles in the 70s alone. They were hammering us by half-time, as *The Munster Express* match report the following week (September 9, 1974) made clear:

Following a first half completely and absolutely dominated by a near rampant Portlaw selection, Mount Sion looked every iota a beaten side as the team trooped off the field at the short whistle. The scoreboard showed the Portlawmen in the commanding position of 2-7 to 0-1 and indeed so well did every member of their side perform in that opening period, that nothing short of a resounding second half win was forecasted.

But all this was reckoned without the unquenchable spirit that is part and parcel of Mount Sion teams. Their selectors made what could only be termed a calculated risk, introducing no fewer than three substitutes for the start of the second half and while drastic remedies called for drastic measures, even this seemed to be stretching the long bow to the limit.

Seamus Power was among our selectors that day. Tony Forristal, the Lord have mercy on him, and Pat O'Grady, who were only coming back from injury at the time and myself – I was also training the team that year – we were all subs that day. Seamus and myself had a chat at half-time and we decided to send both Tony and Pat on.

'And you're going in at full-forward!' Seamus told me in the dressing-room. I was a bit surprised to be honest and I let out a bit of a gasp.

'Do you want to win the f**king match?' said Seamus, in pretty blunt terms. 'Well then, you're going in full-forward for the second half hour.'

I replied, with the touch of shock out of my system by then, 'Alright, so.'

That match was one of the first that Frank, one of our two sons, can remember me playing in.

◄◄◆►►

Frank Morrissey

'SO DAD, TONY and Pat all came out for the start of the second-half. It was one of the first games when you could only bring three subs on instead of five, so to bring the three of them on at the same time was a very ballsy thing to. But Mount Sion were well behind at the time so it probably called for a fairly drastic measure by the management.

Tony and Pat weren't fully fit… my father was 40 by then, he was a selector that year as well, and he knew his time was almost up at that level of hurling. The changes worked and there's no team after coming back like that in a Waterford senior final ever since. It was some way to end his senior career with Mount Sion.

'As a winner.'

◄◄◆►►

WE WERE A transformed team in that second-half, going from 2-7 to 0-1 down to end up winning by 3-8 to 2-10, limiting Portlaw to just three points after the break. The *Munster Express* summed up our comeback well:

All the switches worked like a charm and the big gamble paid off. Tony Forristal brought drive and forceful hurling to a defence heretofore conspicuous by its absence. Pat O'Grady became a dominant figure around the middle of the field and started the recovery by landing a surprise 31st minute goal.

Once again the stylish hurling of Martin Óg Morrissey had its effects around the square and the honours-laden player played no small part in Mount Sion's second half resurgence. In marked contrast to a first half when Mount Sion could only secure a single point and that score coming direct from their outstanding player Pat McGrath, the second half told a different story.

Mount Sionmen hurled for the ball as if their very lives depended upon possession and slowly but ever so effectively, Portlaw's commanding interval lead was whittled away.

◄ ◄ ◆ ► ►

Jim Greene

'I WAS CENTRE-BACK that day, and at half-time they shifted me up to corner-forward. The three changes… and you were only allowed make three changes at the time – including Óg who went in at full-forward – were all made by Seamus Power at half-time. That rarely if ever happened and sure it'd be just as unusual today if all five subs were brought on before the restart.

'From the throw-in, the ball broke to Pat O'Grady who lobbed it in towards goal. Noel O'Sullivan was in goal for Portlaw… to me, he looked terrified, as Óg was hovering, Noel didn't know where to look and the ball ended up in the back of the net. And in the blink of an eye, the whole match swivelled in our favour and we drove on from there.

'It was the best comeback we ever made in any senior final I ever played in. At half-time when the teams were going in, the story goes that Tom Cheasty had murder with the Portlaw lads in the dressing-room… they were cheering as they were going off the field. He told them the match wasn't over by a long shot and he was right.

'But Óg made a massive difference in the second-half, despite having lost a good few yards of pace by then given the miles on the clock. But by God, he was a great bit of stuff.

'A huge inspiration.'

◄ ◄ ◆ ► ►

GOING INTO 1974, I knew it was going to be my last year hurling at senior level. I'd just turned 40… I was tipping away well with the junior team all the while, but it was a real surprise to me when Seamus told me I was coming on for the second-half of the senior final. I'd played full-forward a few times before so it wasn't as if I was a novice going in there or anything.

Now, it's a vast difference to playing at half-back. Your back is to the opposition's goal most of the time as you're moving and hoping that the ball will come your way, before you can think about turning and scoring. But the run of the ball tends to dictate how well things go for you in there.

But the '74 final was one of the good days I had in there and to be part of that winning team was very special. It was a comeback for the ages.

A great way to bow out.

I GENUINELY KNEW my time was up in terms of playing senior hurling. I could feel it… I knew I'd never need anyone else to point that out to me when I had to call it a day. I stopped playing when I knew the time was right… and on my own terms.

I'd have had it no other way.

It might have taken six days to recover from the toughest of matches in my twenties. By the time I was 40, we were talking about weeks at a time in terms of getting a big game out of my limbs. As the Good Book puts it, the spirit was willing but the flesh was weak.

I enjoyed being involved at junior level… it was great to keep the younger players engaged and wanting to improve. In 1974, we won the Eastern Championship and that was very satisfying – I'd missed out on a junior title during my post-minor hiatus away from the club. Naturally, the better junior lads would be drafted into the senior panel when a few of the senior fellas got injured, but that's the nature of the game and still is… you move lads on and hope they rise to the occasion and enjoy long careers at the senior grade.

We'd a winning mentality at junior level… at all levels in the club.

We won four senior football championships too. We were fiercely competitive whatever code we went out in. I remember a Phelan Cup match in Dungarvan against Kilrossanty and we were after beating them already in the championship. In the last 10 minutes, we overpowered them to win the match.

After the match, I noticed one of their players had his boots, togs and stockings rolled up under his arm after he'd got changed… and off he walked out of the pitch. He went straight across the road and fired all his gear into the Colligan.

'I'm not playing f**king football anymore,' he said before he walked off.

He was that disappointed after losing a football match, coming from a part of the county where football was the more widely played game. And while I never flung my gear into the river after losing a hurling match, I felt that same level of disappointment.

It's all very well to tell a fella to 'enjoy the match'. But if you're not winning most times you play, I don't know where you find the enjoyment otherwise. It might well be 'only a game' but when you're stuck into it, when you're in the heat of the moment and when you're used to winning, it's hard to think straight about anything for a while.

And then, after a while you know there'll be another game... and your mind starts to drift to the following Tuesday night training above in the field. And the world keeps turning, even when you're after losing a game.

Mount Sion played fast and open hurling... that was the trademark of the teams I played on. We relished ground hurling then in a way that no modern player could appreciate now... to strike the ball 60 to 70 yards off the ground was a huge part of my game and something I prided myself on. We weren't obsessed with lifting the ball or making a heap of short handpasses. We weren't 100 percent opposed to lifting or handpassing either... we mixed things up well, but the emphasis was always on getting an attack going as soon as possible so as not to let the opposition settle.

Waterford and Mount Sion had very similar approaches, which made sense when you think there were at least six Mount Sion players starting most matches for the county between 1957 and '63.

Neither the club nor the county has been as successful at the same time since then. We expected to win every match we played, so when we lost it was a massive disappointment. Mount Sion could have won 13 in-a-row senior titles and Waterford should definitely have won three All-Irelands during that purple patch.

Granted, the Waterford team I played on won more matches than it lost, and that remains a positive. If the back door system had been in play back then, I think it would have suited us very well. It would have been great to have had that leverage.

It's hard to avoid the 'what if' stuff but despite the trophies we missed out on, it was such an enjoyable time in my life, to hurl alongside so many great players and getting the best out of myself most of the time I played.

Nothing really replaces the feeling of playing and winning once you've taken the boots off for the last time.

◄◄◆►►

Bridie Barron

'WE GREW UP watching Mount Sion, so we were always very attached to them and I followed them wherever they went when Martin was playing. We gave many great days following the club... the hurlers of the present day don't have the same level of skills that they had when Martin and that great Mount Sion team were in their pomp.

Martin had a great run and he has the medals hanging up in his front room to prove that. He was a top class hurler and it was lovely to see him in action for all those years.'

Although playing with Mount Sion was always closest to Martin Óg's heart, despite the occasional difference of opinion, he was also making his name in the biggest stadiums in the country as one of the game's greatest defenders.

« CHAPTER 6 »

Working and Living in Waterford

The future of the Clover Meats Bacon Plant in Waterford remained threatened this week as its 459 employees, members of the IT & GWU maintained their picket on the Christendom factory in support of a pay claim. Mr Eddie Power, Chief Executive of the company, warned all employees in a memorandum last week, that unless they returned to their jobs with the acceptance of a 6% increase and a six month pay pause, the continued existence of the factory will be put at serious risk.

– Waterford News & Star, October 19, 1984

WORK WAS HARD to come by in Waterford after I finished school. There was nothing doing at all for the first two years after I left the doors of Mount Sion behind me. But in 1955, I put in an application to Clover Meats, the big meat processing factory over in Ferrybank and Jim Brennan was the superintendent there at the time. Probably the most interesting thing he said to me during the interview was just as it was finishing up.

'Would you play hurling with us?' he asked me.

'Of course I would,' I instantly replied.

Said Jim straight back to me, 'Great stuff. You'll start on Monday morning, then.' As I knew only too well myself at the time, there were very few job prospects in the town so I realised how lucky I was to get the thumbs up from Jim. Did my hurling ability swing it for me? Well, it clearly didn't do me any harm, let's face it.

I'd end up working there for 29 years before the company went into liquidation, leaving 500 people out of work. Plenty more industrial bombshells would come Waterford's way in the years after that, unfortunately.

BEFORE I GOT the Clover job, I gave about two or three months with the *Waterford News & Star* as a cub reporter but it didn't take too long for me to figure out that journalism and myself didn't go hand in glove. Reporting just didn't come too naturally to me. Clover Meats did. Everyone hired in there went in initially for a three-month trial on eight pounds a week. Now you wouldn't have been doing a whole lot with that kind of money… it might have stretched to a pack of 20 Players and a box of matches, but that was about it!

Clover had plenty of good hurlers on the payroll, mostly drawn from Waterford and Kilkenny. You had Mullinavat's John Sutton, who won his All-Ireland medal in the Kilkenny team that got the better of us in 1957, and John Barron from Morrisson's Road, who played in all three All-Ireland finals that we reached from 1957 to '63. There were plenty of other fellas in the panel who had played inter-county at minor and junior level, so they had their wits about them out on a hurling field, including Paddy Buggy, who later served as GAA President in the Centenary Year of 1984. They were a great bunch.

There was Seán Fleming, who played minor for Waterford, Mickey Murphy who played senior, and then you had Paddy Hogan and Neddie Dwyer… and Mickey Fitzgerald, the best Kilkenny hurler who never won an inter-county All-Ireland senior medal – at least that's what he used to tell us – and always with a smile.

The toughest matches I played were in the Factory League against fellas from my own club. We always had a go at each other. Nothing used to be ever held back. But between training and the Factory League, once the final whistle was blown, what had gone on in the field stayed right there. Five minutes after a match, you could be going for a walk with one of the fellas you were after hitting and that's just the way it was meant to be. There was none of us interested in 'afters'.

It was probably the making of us.

The first-time hurling that people younger than me would describe as long ago – the stuff there's only newsreel footage of – it looks fantastic to me compared to fellas today, 10 or 11 of them around the ball and they trying to pick it up, just arseing around. And the small hurleys they use now, sure that's the reason they can't play ground hurling because they can't reach down and pull on it.

I'd say if I was playing today, I reckon I'd last about five minutes.

The first year I was working at Clover, we won the Factory League Munster Championship and it was a great competition to hurl in. After the Munster Championship fell through not too long after that, we ended up playing in the Leinster Championship thanks to the efforts of Sean Williams… and we won that several times. More importantly, we won two All-Ireland titles as well, so if you were working in Clover at the time and you also happened to be hurling senior for either Waterford or Kilkenny, this was a very successful period altogether.

And we had a great time playing for Clover. We really enjoyed it. We'd hire a bus to head off to the matches, and after every match we'd head for the pub for a sing-song. It was definitely a more relaxed feeling than you'd have playing for the club or the county, but once we were out on the field we always gave it our all.

When that first ball was thrown in, all your thoughts were on the match and that was it.

CLOVER MEATS WAS almost four miles from my front door.

I cycled to and from work every day, six days a week, which meant that I was fairly fit the whole time. That was on top of training on Tuesday and Thursday evenings when you'd have the sugar knocked out of you. But I was half-fit, so to speak, before I went into the field at all.

The only lads you'd see cycling to training nowadays are youngsters, and sure you'd only see a handful of adults walking to a nearby shop now to get a carton of milk, a few cigarettes or a newspaper.

The modern inter-county hurler is certainly fitter now than any of us were – Philly Grimes, mind you, was a natural athlete – thanks to diets, ice baths and gym schedules and so on. But I doubt if they're as hardy as we were on a day-to-day basis. Going back 60 years, life was harder for someone of 20 than it is for most 20-year-olds nowadays.

That's just a fact, plain and simple.

For a time, there was talk of putting Clover Meats into the Kilkenny Senior Championship but that fell through and I don't mind saying, taking my lineage into account, I'd have liked to have hurled in it. However, on the whole, I still think the Waterford championship was stronger than Kilkenny's at the time.

Bennettsbridge were the dominant team in Kilkenny during that era and even though Mount Sion obviously had that great run of nine in-a-row, there were good Erin's Own and Ballygunner teams on this side of the Suir. I found the Kilkenny players to be more laid back about their hurling than us Waterford fellas. And that's not meant as a criticism.

Nothing seemed to ruffle them at all... when they made a mistake, they just dusted it off and got on with things, whereas a good few of us in white and blue used to take a lot longer to get over something not going our way. Kilkenny have won their share of MacCarthy Cups post-1959. Twenty-two, in fact.

Yet here we are, still waiting for someone in our colours to follow Frankie Walsh up the Hogan Stand steps.

There probably wasn't as much emphasis on winning at that time as there is now... sure there's fellas playing inter-county now and a good few of them look like they've forgotten how to smile during a match. All these gym sessions and so on might be unavoidable nowadays because everyone is committed to these programmes, but I wonder how many of them genuinely enjoy what they're doing?

Will they have as many good memories about the game 40 or 50 years from now, as fellas my age had from their playing days? I'm not convinced they will, to be honest.

I'll probably be dismissed as an old-timer looking back on his own era with rose-tinted glasses but when I look at inter-county matches now on the television, this is what I see... 10 to 12 fellas hovering over the ball, as I've said... trying to poke at it or pick it up. That was what you saw in junior hurling during my time.

And questions have to be asked about the modern ball. If we'd been using today's ball when I hurled, Ollie Walsh would have been scoring points from puck-outs for Kilkenny.

When the axe swung on Clover Meats, jobs weren't plentiful in Waterford, just as they hadn't been when I began working there. After the factory closed and all hope of a takeover or revival petered out, I spent the following two years working for the GAA in Walsh Park for two and a half days a week, looking after the pitch and doing smaller jobs around the ground. Then I worked for Delta, a security company in Ferrybank. But that work wound up when Bell Lines folded in 1997 and that was the end of my full-time work.

When my brother was stuck, I used to give him a hand driving one of his coal lorries, doing deliveries. I spent about a year counting the bales of hay going onto the cattle boats on the South Quays in Waterford, but that all stopped when the cattle exports ended. After that, I was what was known as 'a man of leisure', not that I took much pleasure from that.

I'd like to have kept working. That's what I was used to and I was happy on it. I used to be in Clover Meats for 7am every morning. During the winters, we used to be very busy and we worked two nights a week, often until 10pm… it really was a great job. It was such a pity it fell through.

I ended up as a charge hand in the 'bailing room' as we used to call it where we sent out all the bacon and I got to know a lot of people through the job, including a lot of people from the North who drove lorries. Between bacon and pork, we were kept busy.

Those were the good old days, with plenty of good-humoured slagging on the factory floor but sure we took it all with a pinch of salt.

IN MY YOUTH, Waterford City's attractions more than held my interest. The done thing at the time was to go for a walk around the town in the night time when all the shops were closed. My usual route was Broad Street, Michael Street, The Mall and The Quay… roughly a triangle if you plotted it on a map. We'd walk that maybe three or four times before heading home for a bit of supper before bed. Of course, there were also the nights when you'd go to the pictures at the Regal, the Savoy, the Theatre Royal and the Coliseum… that was in behind the Tower Hotel.

We called the woman that ran the Coliseum, Olive, as in 'Olive Oyl' from the *Popeye* cartoon, and we used to have great gas down there.

Sometimes, we used to bring pigeons in under our coats, into the cinema… and then we left them off to fly around the auditorium and people used to be afraid of their lives of the birds flying around! We had great times down there.

I was a big admirer of 'The Duke', John Wayne, and I used to love going to see the films he topped the bill in. There were some great old westerns and cowboy films like *Hopalong Cassidy* with William Boyd, along with Johnny Mack Brown and Gene Autry… they were another few of my favourites.

The films used to run as serials back then; you'd see one part one Saturday and then the next part would be screened the following Saturday. At the end of nearly every one of these, 'The Chap', the good guy in the serial, he either tended to get shot or fall off his horse.

But then the following week, there he was again, miraculously still alive.

Talk about the magic of the movies.

Jack O'Neill, a great local historian, remembered such nights out in his book, *A Waterford Miscellany*:

Another type of film featured on occasions was an early horror film, usually with Bela Lugosi or Lon Chaney as the evil character. They appeared as Frankenstein or as Dracula and Werewolves, and were responsible for the premature emptying of many a weak bladder in the seats as the patrons screamed with fright.

Some patrons even hid under the seats as the terror stalked the female lead or wrapped themselves around their boyfriend. Why they always seemed to be out to catch the lady baffled the terrified patrons. These films usually ended with the sun rising, birds singing and the hero and heroine embracing over the dead remains of the spectre.

Leaving the cinema, there would have been the odd one having difficulty walking in wet underwear but, at least, there was the consolation that good had triumphed… so all was well…

During the interval between the first showing and the feature film, the lights were switched on in the house and girls from the cinema shops attached to the Savoy and Regal paraded along the aisles with trays of chocolates, cigarettes and fruit suspended with a belt across the shoulders. Filmgoers were encouraged to buy while the interval lasted.

You usually had two films being shown… firstly, a short film followed by a break and then a 'trailer' as it's now known, which would show a clip of the film that would be shown in a week's time. And then that took you into the main feature of the night.

You'd head in for seven o'clock, you'd be out at ten and that'd be the night's entertainment, sometimes with fleeing pigeons included. I don't remember much in the way of news reels being projected in the Waterford cinemas at the time.

In terms of socialising, my weekends didn't revolve around drink. It never had too big a hold on me; I could go six or 12 months without having a pint or even going near a public house. In hindsight, I think I was lucky in that sense. I remember more than one fella saying to me they wish they could be a bit more like me when it came to my levels of moderation.

Over the years, I knew more than a few alcoholics around the town. They just couldn't get by without the bloody stuff. I was never in that boat and I'm glad of that now. Looking back, not being a big drinker might well have had some unforeseen consequences for me. But every big decision that I made, be it about hurling or when it came to my family or work, I stand over them all to this day.

WE'VE BEEN LIVING in 'Banna', just off Hennessy's Road in Waterford City, for more than 40 years… and we built it and furnished it for about £4,500 at the time. We called it after Banna Strand in County Kerry, which I visited more than once over the years and it's such a beautiful place. And of course, it will be forever associated with Roger Casement, who landed there off a German U-Boat in April 1916, was detained by the British soon afterwards and hanged for high treason in London in August of that same year.

It was the last of the rofab (precast concrete panel) houses to be built around here and sure it would be 50 times more expensive, at least, to build what we have on this site nowadays. When it came to building or financing new houses, back then it was most definitely a case of the good old days. I feel very sorry for anyone trying to make a start now when it comes to a house.

I can remember plots along the road here, up to 70 or 80 of them, where fellas used to set potatoes mainly. And I can go back even further, to a time when there were no houses here at all. Then during the Second World War, there were flat-roofed houses built opposite where we're living now and they were only meant to be temporary… and it wasn't that long ago that they were finally pulled down and replaced by the houses over there now.

There's a lot of old people living along here now; we were all young when we moved in and built our homes here, so it's a very settled place. The neighbours have always looked out for each other, and that counts for a lot as you get older. A decent bunch.

A good few lads around here played hurling and when the Roanmore club started up in 1970, a lot of them ended up in the sky blue jersey. This part of the city had been a cradle for Mount Sion up until then, so the likes of Kieran Delahunty and Noelie Crowley, who won back-to-back senior championships in 1989 and '90 and played for Waterford in the 1989 Munster final, had they been born a few decades earlier, they'd have been Mount Sion men!

The foundation of Roanmore was a big drain on Mount Sion and there's no getting away from the fact that we lost many top class hurlers to the city's newest club. The topsoil that came out of the Waterford Crystal site when the factory was built in Kilbarry – up the road here from my front door – all went into Roanmore's first pitch.

At least it was put to good use. Roanmore have made a resurgence in the last few years and the matches with Mount Sion have that historic edge to them, even now, over 50 years later. I doubt if that will ever fade.

Martin Óg and Eamon (above) at the beach. Brigid and Martin Óg settling into family life in Waterford.

The young couple enjoying their married life.

« CHAPTER 7 »

The County Call and Some Big What Ifs...

DECLAN GOODE, WHO was then secretary of the Waterford County Board, posted me a note to let me know I'd been selected for the Waterford senior hurling panel. It was 1955. There'd be a little instruction on the note sent out to each player... urging any of us that got the nod to be fit for whatever games were coming up.

Collective training wasn't much of a thing at that stage at inter-county level and it only began to gather pace during my time – Kerry was the only established team in either code that was training together by the mid-50s. But if you were training on a Tuesday night, then in all likelihood you were training the following Thursday, and that's what became the pattern.

I was hoping to get the slip of paper from Declan. And I'm not going to lie, I was expecting it. I was after spending four years on the Munster Colleges' panel and I had played three years minor with Waterford. I was reckoned to be one of the best young hurlers in the county at the time and being on the victorious Harty Cup team was a big feather in my cap.

I felt I was ready to make the step up.

Before I got selected for the senior panel, I remember playing a match above in Tourin, one of the most westerly pitches in Waterford at the time. And would you be believe, there were five lads named Fives on their starting team – sure it was 25 against 15!

One of them came over to me after the match and said that if I kept playing like that, I was bound to end up on Waterford's senior panel. To have someone at the opposite end of the county telling me something like that was very encouraging. I mightn't have been someone who was particularly lacking in confidence, but I'm as grateful for a bit of encouragement as anyone.

Going back even further in time, I remember hurling out on the street and Stephen Greene, godfather of future Sion and Waterford great, Jim Greene, said to my father, 'Well, Ned, we'll be looking at that fella hurling in Croke Park some day!'

I never forgot the impression those words made on me when I was only a young fella.

Stephen wasn't wrong, thank God.

ONE OF MY first senior appearances for the county was below in the Athletic Grounds in Cork on a Friday evening… where Páirc Uí Chaoimh now stands. Mick Healy, a fellow Mount Sion man and a substitute in the 1948 All-Ireland winning Waterford panel, was playing the same night. In fact, he's the only fella I can remember playing with that day.

Being a Fast Day, as it was at that time, meant we had fish on the menu that evening. Paddy Barry and Christy Ring were in the Cork team that night and that was the first time I saw 'Ringy' in the flesh. Unlike today, we'd no idea who'd be in the opposition's starting fifteen until we were out on the field – but there was Christy Ring, by then approaching his mid-thirties but with almost another decade of inter-county hurling still in front of him.

The late John A Murphy, well known to older readers of *The Irish Examiner* and *Waterford News & Star* wrote the following of Ring for the *Dictionary of Irish Biography*:

A perfectionist, he practised long hours daily, alone or with teammates, to develop and maintain his skills. He always carried a camán and sliothar in the cab of his lorry and would practise in fields and against walls at intervals throughout his working day. A non-smoker and non-drinker, he revelled in hard training, and maintained himself in peak fitness throughout his career.

Confident in his ability, he did not suffer from false modesty in his estimation of his own genius. He once remarked that modesty was not to deny the ability that one knew oneself to have, but to know one's own ability while also knowing one's weaknesses.

I never thought of Ring as being Cú-Chulainn's successor, or of him being the greatest hurler of his generation. It just wasn't in my make-up to think of someone I was hurling against in those terms. To be honest, it never bothered me who I was playing against and I never elevated any opponent above the other. I'd a job to do no matter who it was I was marking or might cross my path.

A few years ago, I was interviewed over in Ballybricken to talk about, you guessed it… hurling, and Ring came into conversation. Ringy was probably the best bit of stuff that ever played the game. There was a chap from Wexford in the audience that night and after the interview had finished, he told me, 'I saw Ring in his early days and, as far as I was concerned, he was only a mediocre player'.

It struck me as a fairly unique observation of Ring. But the man himself said, 'I don't want to be the best hurler in Ireland… I want to play the best hurling in Ireland.' Christy was outstanding on the field and a gentleman off it. Another taken far too soon.

To begin with, I was mainly a substitute on the Waterford senior panel when I moved up from minor and my first championship match was against Limerick in 1955, a game we lost by a goal (4-5 to 3-5) up in the Gaelic Grounds. That particular Limerick team was known as 'Mackey's Greyhounds'… the great Mick Mackey was their trainer and they were renowned for their pace, and they had some smashing players like Vivian Cobbe and Dermot Kelly. They lost to a great Wexford team in the All-Ireland semi-final, featuring Nicky Rackard and Tim Flood, and they ended up winning that year's final against Galway.

I came in off the bench, and I knew I made a good impression that day. The next time I played I was in at corner-forward, but then the next match after that I was on the sideline. I wasn't too happy about it.

◄◄◆►►

Bridie Barron

'WHEN MARTIN WAS named in the Waterford senior panel, it was a great moment for him and for all the family. And my goodness, he didn't half leave a mark once he got that county jersey on his back. He was always a very confident fella out on the field… there was hardly ever a game he played in which he didn't know exactly what he had to do.

'He was so committed to hurling and whoever he played alongside. But he was always a bit different off the field, that bit more reserved.'

◄◄◆►►

WE WERE DOWN to play Limerick in Walsh Park later on that year. Well, I was at home in bed that morning when a knock came on the door. My mother opened the door and there was Seamus Power standing there, the Lord have mercy on him.

'Is Óg there?' he asked.

'He's in bed,' said my mother.

'We're playing a match,' he said back, and I hopped out of the bed when I heard him and came down to the front door.

'Seamus, I'm not going!' I said.

'Why?' he replied, and then I rattled off all the matches I'd played well in. 'I'm browned off with being sent in corner-forward and then getting dropped again.' So off Seamus went and he must have conveyed a message because some time after that we played Tipperary above in Walsh Park and I was named at left full-back.

John Barron had been shifted out to centre-half-back where he was marking Mick Ryan from Roscrea, who'd played on the three in-a-row All-Ireland winning Tipp team from 1949 to '51. After 15 minutes, John was after hitting a single ball while I hit every ball that came into me. Not too long after that, I was shifted out to centre-back and I never left the half-back line again after that for Waterford. I put Mick Ryan in my pocket and that was the day I cemented my place in the starting team with the majority of my time spent at left half back.

I was delighted to be playing senior for Waterford and I was excited about it in my own way... I wasn't skipping up the street and whistling about it, but it was a great feeling and a huge honour for me. You'd think about all the fellas who'd be telling you afterwards what you ought to have done during a match, when there'd only be a small fraction of them ever after wearing the jersey.

I knew whose words mattered when it came to that... the rest just went in one ear and out the other. But I took the whole experience with a grain of salt – after all, starting off, I could never be too certain that I'd be playing the next day.

I never took it for granted.

The panel I came into still featured a handful of the 1948 All-Ireland winning team, including Johnny O'Connor, Mick Hayes and Eddie Carew. John Keane, who played for the senior football championship winning Mount Sion side in 1955 aged 38, was a few years retired from the inter-county scene by then but there was no Waterford supporter, let alone a Mount Sion man, who couldn't think of 1948 without thinking of John Keane, Waterford's sole representative on the hurling Team of the Millennium. But again, a little like Ring, when you're in and around figures of that stature, sometimes you're a little blinded to just what an impact and contribution to the game John made. Then as the years clock up, your appreciation for what these men did certainly grows. And that was definitely the case with John as, in my younger years, I really didn't realise just how good he was.

The *Mount Sion Club Souvenir Record* in 1974 described John Keane in the following terms:

John ranks with the all-time greats of hurling. He is to Mount Sion and Waterford what Mick Mackey is to Ahane and Limerick, Christy Ring to Glen Rovers and Cork, Lory Meagher to Tullaroan and Kilkenny. He remains for many of us a man apart, a man who in his physique, his character, his personality, his sportsmanship, his sheer artistry as a hurler and his enduring loyalty to the game he graced for so long, was the very epitome of Mount Sion's and Waterford's hurling spirit.'

You'd find no-one still alive who knew John who'd disagree with any of that.

John was an outstanding bit of stuff for club and county. He was a big man on the field and few fellas ever took a ball off him once he was in possession of it. Larry Fanning, who played full-back with Mount Sion, was once asked to pick his all-time Mount Sion fifteen and I met him a few days after he picked it, in a shop in town.

'I just couldn't put you in front of John Keane at centre-half-back,' Larry told me. 'But you'd have to be on the best Mount Sion team ever having watched you since you were a young fella… so I put you at left full-back.'

Now that's where I started playing hurling so at least Larry had put me in a position that I'd actually played in, unlike some of the All Star selectors over the years. To be picked by Larry on that team was something I was very proud of and to be considered second best to John Keane was then, and always will be, a feather in my cap.

John set the bar high for all who succeeded him with both Mount Sion and Waterford. To have someone I respected as much as Larry saying I got somewhere near the level John is about the best praise I could ever have received.

◄◄◆►►

Pat Fanning

'ÓG WOULDN'T BE the most modest fella in the world, but he has always spoken about himself and how good he was in a very affable way. You could only take to him for speaking the way he does... he's always had a very distinctive, charming way about him.

'The funny thing is, that for all his great qualities as a player, he was probably one of the laziest men to ever play inter-county hurling when it came to training. Jack Furlong was the Waterford masseur at the time... he was a lorry driver for John Hearn's, the ironmongers on The Quay, he was an Erin's Own man, he always wore a soft cap, he was a great character and he was also stone deaf.

'But his favourite thing to do in Walsh Park was to look after Óg and he'd a full time job doing it. The minute Óg would go into training, the first thing he'd have to get was the rubdown from Jack... and the wintergreen was always liberally applied.

'And when Óg walked out onto the field, you could smell the wintergreen off him... and a lot of the early running drills might have been done by then. That's the way he operated, but it worked for him.

'And when it came to playing, there were few days that Óg didn't deliver for Waterford. He was an amazing hurler. He had the wristwork that would equal Christy Ring.

'He was centre-back for Waterford during a time when other strong hurling counties had bigger, taller men in the same position, such as Billy Rackard in Wexford, who loved catching the incoming ball. Óg rarely if ever caught the ball. He'd wait for the ball to come all the way in on the ground to him, then he'd hit it on the drop and drive it the length of the field.

'He was a brilliant exponent of the drop shot and he was a great advocate of ground hurling, and when he had to take the ball in hand, he was always clever with his distribution. When you think about that Waterford team, there were no particularly tall men on it... Philly Grimes was probably the tallest at 5'10" or 11". Tom Cheasty had a strong upper body but he was no taller than I am, and then you'd Seamus Power, Frankie Walsh, Larry Guinan and so on, all in and around 5' 8".

And when you think Wexford at that time had Ned Wheeler and the Rackards, all over six feet tall, it's amazing Waterford could compete and beat teams over a sustained period. It was a team built on speed, skill and fitness... and Óg was at the heart of that team.'

◄ ◄ ◆ ► ►

I WAS VERY keen to take possession of a starting position for the county and nail it down for as long as I could. I always felt I had enough hurling in me to do just that. I felt I'd accomplished that by 1957 and I had my hands on the jersey until '64 when we lost a high-scoring Munster semi-final to Cork in Thurles, going down by one point in a 4-10 to 5-6 defeat.

That loss was effectively marked the end of that great Waterford team's era. It was a special team to be part of. Great and all as the 1959 All-Ireland win was, we left at least two All-Irelands behind us in 1957 and '63. And I wasn't the only one of the group who thought that. Raymond Smith captured our mood well in the chapter he devoted to 'Waterford's Finest Team' in his book, *The Hurling Immortals*.

'*What won it for us in 1959 was the loss of the 1957 crown*', said John Keane. '*The 1957 defeat made our players more steady and they did not make the same mistake twice.*'

'*I always maintain that we should have won that 1957 final,*' said John Barron. '*The team was playing hurling with great fluency, particularly Seamus Power and Philly Grimes and it was a big shock when Kilkenny got there by a point.*'

IN 1957, WE BEAT Limerick by 4-12 to 5-5 in Cork to advance to a Munster final against Cork in Thurles. For that final, Willie John Daly was brought back into Cork's starting team to play centre-forward against us. The story that went round that day was that Paddy Greene – All Star winner Jim's father – was sitting on the sideline in Thurles and he was surrounded by Cork fellas talking about what Willie John was going to do during the match.

Well, we ended up winning that day by 1-11 to 1-6 to take the Munster title for the first time since the great 1948 team's success. At full-time, Paddy got up, turned around and addressed the Cork men with a wide grin on his face.

'Well, there ye have it now, lads. After all yer talk… Willie John didn't do anything!' After that, we beat Galway by 4-12 to 0-11 to advance to a final and a meeting with our Kilkenny neighbours. It was the beginning of a great rivalry between the two counties.

In that period, we also lost two National League finals along with the two All-Ireland finals – both to Tipperary in 1959 (by 0-15 to 0-7) and in 1961 (by 6-6 to 4-9). No two ways about it, we had a good old team but I still don't think one All-Ireland, one league, an Oireachtas title and three Munster Championships reflected just how good we actually were.

In saying that, I think we were probably short of one outstanding player, the fella who would have made all the difference in tight matches.

As I've said already, I still look back on both the 1957 and '63 All-Ireland finals with a huge sense of frustration. We really should have won three All-Irelands during that spell. We were more than good enough to have done just that. The size of the crowd in any of the finals I played in, be it Munster or All-Ireland, never really came into it for me.

It was all about the ball, where I'd put it next and how I'd try and keep my opposite number quiet. You have to play the game. You can't allow it to become an occasion… sure you'd have been better off up in the stands if that's the way you were thinking.

Of course, the 1957 final stands alone in the history of the GAA given the presence of an additional 'player' in Kilkenny colours during the pre-match parade. The actor John Gregson was starring in a movie called *Rooney*, a story about a binman who hurled for his county – and Barry Fitzgerald and Noel Purcell, big names at the time, featured in the cast. Now, Gregson ended up in Kilkenny colours, but he'd asked to parade with us first.

The thought in the Waterford camp at the time was that there was no place in our parade line at Croke Park on the first Sunday in September for a fella that didn't play hurling… so our answer was no. So then Gregson went into their dressing-room, asked the Kilkenny fellas the same question and they said yes… so he paraded with them.

He pulled a fast one on us!

By the way, about a fortnight after the 1957 All-Ireland final, we were back up in Croke Park for, would you believe it, a few more shots with John Gregson for *Rooney*. Now we only got told about this around four days before the scenes were shot.. we'd no idea we'd be going back up to Dublin right after we'd lost the All-Ireland.

But off we went and we ended up making a weekend out of it. So all the Waterford and Kilkenny players were there again, not knowing we were foreshadowing the real replay we'd end up playing two years later. Well, it took Gregson about three-quarters of an hour to score a goal... it took him nearly as long to solo with the ball, so it's safe to say his acting skills outshone his hurling ability.

I was still pretty down in the dumps about the All-Ireland, so to be back in Croke Park so soon after losing, was a bit strange alright. But we got paid for it, over 60 pounds each and I earning only eight pounds a week at the time... so I reckon we must have been the first inter-county players to get payment from appearing at GAA headquarters.

I felt like a millionaire coming home that evening.

We were in control of most of the actual 1957 final and then Kilkenny's Mick Kenny, who ended the day with 2-5, scored a goal with eight minutes remaining to leave us just a point ahead. At one stage in the second-half we led by 3-10 to 2-7 and we really should have seen it out. Seán Clohosey put over the equaliser with five minutes remaining, before Mick Kelly scored what turned out to be the winning point.

There's not many teams score 3-12 in an All-Ireland final and end up losing. But that was our fate on the day Kilkenny lifted Liam MacCarthy for the 13th time.

The *Cork Examiner* match report (September 2, 1957) offered a very fair assessment of the previous day's events, even though it's hardly a day Waterford supporters have reminisced over:

In the splendour of its hurling, in the breathtaking uncertainty of its relentless vigour and excitement, the 1957 All-Ireland Senior Hurling Final at Croke Park yesterday will long be remembered and always with pleasure. It was at once a victory of highest courage and magnificent tragedy. Kilkenny triumphed when failure seemed their lot; Waterford failed when a triumph seemed assured. But no Decies follower need recall this wonderful hour with regret, for it was proved without a shadow of a doubt

that from the barren years which have yielded only one All-Ireland title, has come a
Decies team to take its place among the mightiest in the game.

◄ ◄ ◆ ▷ ►

Bridie Barron

'WE WERE WORKING in Clover Meats and we were just dying to beat Kilkenny. The childhood affection for Kilkenny went firmly into the back seat whenever Waterford played them. John Sutton, Willie Murphy and Mickey 'Browley' Walsh worked there at the time and they played for Kilkenny in 1957, while Martin and John Barron were in the Waterford team.

'Funny enough, Mickey Browley ended up marrying Noline Mulcahy in the early 60s so he transferred to Mount Sion from Slieverue and came on a sub for Waterford in the 1963 All-Ireland final, having played against Waterford in the '57 and '59 finals. So that only added to the excitement on the shopfloor ahead of the match.

'It ended up being a very close match and we were roaring bawling at full-time. After the match, I remember saying to Martin, "There's only one thing you can do now… grit your teeth and the next time ye meet Kilkenny in the All-Ireland final, make sure the cup is coming over the bridge with ye". Luckily, they didn't have to wait too long to put that wrong to right – unlike the wait we've all been living with since.

'But 1959 was so special. When Seamus Power scored his goal in the first match, I really thought we were going to win. But it went to a second day and we ended up winning it with a bit to spare. My heart almost leapt out of my chest at full-time… my mother thought I was going to faint with the excitement.

'We didn't see Martin then until all the players were back home in the city. God, it was a great day and the scenes on The Quay were unbelievable with tens of thousands of people out to welcome them home. But they should have won more than one All-Ireland.

'There's no getting away from that.'

◄ ◄ ◆ ▷ ►

HOWEVER TOUGH IT was to lose in 1957, in many ways, a harder experience was to come six years later. In 1963, to score 6-8 and still lose remains hard to credit. Eddie Keher scored 11 frees that day and we barely got a free the same day.

I remember Seamus Cleere, who was playing right half-back for Kilkenny, catching the ball three times in the run-up to one point and the ref never pulled him for it. Seán Clohosey was marked by Mick Flannery that day. Clohosey clearly fouled Flan. The referee blew the whistle and signalled a free for Kilkenny. We couldn't believe it.

Clohosey turned around and said to Flan, 'We're after getting something there that we shouldn't be getting.' Players always know.

Those two decisions swung it for Kilkenny that day, I think.

Ned Power had a very tough day in goal in 1963. Goalkeeper is the least forgiving position on the pitch when things don't go for you and they certainly didn't go for Ned against Kilkenny that afternoon. Ned was asked about the 1963 final in an interview he gave entirely as gaeilge in 1994.

'It was a disastrous day. I remember it well,' he said.

'I was injured in the opening minutes. One of my ribs was broken. I wasn't able to breathe in properly… I couldn't hit the sliotar out properly. So of course, I couldn't stop the sliotar properly. We were unlucky in many ways in that match.

'At the same time, it shows what a powerful team we had when we scored six goals and eight points against Ollie Walsh. Eddie Keher was so sharp that day. He could put the sliotar over the bar without looking. He scored 17 points that day. He also scored a goal.

'He also gave me a poke in the rib that was broken. I wasn't too thankful to him.'

Frankie Walsh frequently recalled the events of 1963 at the many functions he attended, when he spoke so well. 'Percy Flynn came on for Ned in the second-half; we made changes in the backline and the half-forward line. But our full-forward line that day was just superb. Seamus Power scored three goals, and he'd been in bed all week before that with the 'flu.

'Seamus Cleere won Man of the Match and he deserved it. He'd a great game and that was no surprise as he was a great player.'

Frankie took a slightly different view from myself when it came to that 1957-63 period. He didn't see us as underachievers.

'I wouldn't think that way at all about that team,' he insisted. 'You have to remember there were lots of great teams around at the time… it's often been said to me by different people from around the country that that Waterford team should have won more, that we should have won three or four All-Irelands. And maybe we should have.

'I always thought 1957 and '63 were the ones we should have won. In 1959, I thought we played well in the first match, but didn't play as well in the replay and won. And when you win an All-Ireland by eight points, I don't think any of us were about to start complaining about how we'd played.

'We just had the bit of luck we needed that day to win.

'We had some great games with Cork and Tipp during those years. Kilkenny and Wexford were very strong… sure Wexford had a great side at the time. The standard was very high across a few counties. Seán Clohosey came down to speak at the team's 25th anniversary in 1984 and he said had he got the chance to play for any (other) team it would have been the Waterford team of 1959, which was as good a compliment as could be made about that team.'

Tom Cheasty, one of 10 who started both the 1959 and '63 finals, was as annoyed as any of us for years afterwards about '63. Back in 2002, following Waterford's first Munster senior crown in 39 years, he said, 'We'd been there three times as winners of the Munster Championship (between 1957 and '63) and I thought we might need eight, maybe 10 years before we might challenge again.

'I didn't think we'd have to wait too long to win a Munster title again. In 1963, we'd won the Munster, we won the league and we'd won the Oireachtas the year before, which was a fairly important competition at the time. We lost the All-Ireland final yet we scored six goals.

'You have to remember it was only a 60-minute game back then, so to score so well and still lose was disappointing from our point of view.'

AT PADDY BUGGY'S funeral in Slieverue (in 2013), I got talking to Johnny McGovern, one of Paddy's Kilkenny teammates and a great clubman with Bennettsbridge for many a year, about the 1963 All-Ireland final. 'If you'd got two more balls that day, Óg, we'd have lost and you'd have two All-Ireland winners' medals today rather than one,' he told me.

He maintained that the ball I'd been sending into our forwards was after producing a lot of our scores that day. Eddie Keher got all those frees. Of the

6-8 we scored, only one of ours was from a free, scored by Philly Grimes. Now if you can find a team in the last hundred years or even further back that won an All-Ireland with only one point from a free, good luck to you. Then again, there are probably fewer that scored 6-8 from play in an All-Ireland final that ended up losing the game.

I'm fully convinced that the ref made an absolute hames of the game on us that day. To have one team being awarded multiples of frees and the other team ended up getting just made no sense to me whatsoever. Sure there had to be something wrong there. For me, 1963 really was an All-Ireland that got away from us.

We were more than good enough to win that day. And there'd have been far less talk about 1959 if we had, naturally.

Don't get me wrong, I'll always be proud of what that Waterford team won and I can't imagine I'd ever grow weary of talking about the great hurlers I soldiered with. But we should have won more.

That, in many ways, is the history of Waterford hurling at inter-county level. But that, in its own way, all these years later, makes 1959 so special. The achievement of winning that All-Ireland title remains something that the few of us still alive who hurled that day take great pride in.

And so we should.

Martin Óg came up against the very best early in his career, including Christy Ring (right) and Eddie Keher.

« CHAPTER 8 »

Kings for One Day

Hail Waterford, the new holders of the All-Ireland hurling title. Champions among champions are these white and blue clad men of the Decies. For this second championship, which they won so splendidly in Croke Park yesterday and now take across the Suir for the second time, must surely stand apart as the greatest by far of the 72 championships that have now been played in the 75 years of the GAA. With justifiable pride they can wear their All-Ireland crown. As no other team before them has done – they have won it in the hardest possible manner in an extended championship. For on the way to this triumph they have defeated Galway, Tipperary, Cork and now Kilkenny – counties that have between them taken 51 of the All-Ireland titles.

– Mick Dunne (*The Irish Press*, October 5, 1959)

THINKING ABOUT the All-Ireland winning team I played on, I knew some of the fellas really well, in particular the Mount Sion complement, but others not as well as I should have. And as the years have passed, given all the hands we've shaken at many a funeral and all the stories shared afterwards, I wish I'd known them all a bit better.

We did something very special and no team from this county at this grade has emulated us since. I was proud to be a teammate to all of them and even prouder to have been lifelong friends with a good few of them. What great days we had together.

The men of 1959.

Kings for one day.

NED POWER (GOALKEEPER, TALLOW)

NED OCCUPIED THE most important position in our team. No-one has a bigger responsibility on a hurling or football field than the goalkeeper. You can make a mistake at corner-back or corner-forward and a good deal of the time you can get away with that error, or someone else can clear it up for you.

But you've no such luxury when you've got the No 1 on your back – one slip of the wrists back there can cost your team a goal. But don't forget that the ball has a long way to travel to work its way into the goalkeeper in the first place and when things don't work out well for a 'keeper, sometimes the role played by the backs in front of him tends to get overlooked.

Ned was a very good shot-stopper but he was probably more comfortable dealing with the high ball than the ball struck off the surface.

I played and trained a couple of times a week with Ned but that's not the same as spending what I'd describe as proper time with someone and getting to know him. The time we were together was all about hurling.

Ned was from Tallow, the other end of the county in comparison to myself. Had he been hurling for Mount Sion, sure we'd have probably seen each other a few times every week away from training since, in all likelihood, we'd only been living a few doors or streets apart... passing each other on Barrack Street and stopping for a chat or even popping into one of each other's houses for a game of cards.

In my time, you stuck with your own crowd when you were having a meal or travelling to matches, the same way Ned would have done with the lads from the west of the county. But I look back now and I wish I'd got to know Ned and a few other fellas from the panel back then better than I did.

Before you cross the River Bride into Tallow, when driving from Lismore, you'll see a statue of Ned there, captured for all time, famously plucking a sliotar from high in the sky. It's based on a famous photograph taken by Louis McMonagle during the 1962 Munster semi-final against Cork. In the photo Christy Ring is pictured tangling with Tom Cunningham while Ned towers above them all.

Ned deserved the honour of that statue on his home sod.

Ned died on November 15, 2007.

JOE HARNEY (CORNER-BACK, BALLYDURN)

JOE WAS A tough bit of stuff. He feared no-one.

It was only in recent years that I found out that when we were playing Cork in one of our many Munster Championship meetings that Joe actually hurled with a broken ankle. He tore off the plaster of paris before the match and went out and marked Christy Ring, and played the whole match.

Few kept Ring scoreless in a Munster final but Joe did that in 1959. It was only a few years ago when we were having a chat about hurling and he was talking to me about a Ballydurn/Ballygunner junior championship match, and Ballygunner were after being hugely talked up leading up to the match. Joe told his teammates, 'We'll give them plenty of the hurley and we'll win it'. Ballydurn won.

Joe made his championship debut for Waterford in 1957 against Limerick in Cork and himself and Batty Foley were the only junior club players in the county panel when they got the call-up.

Describing Joe's performance in the 1959 All-Ireland replay, 'Deiseach', the *Waterford News & Star* columnist, wrote:

What of this quiet man from Ballydurn, the man who was faulted by so many in the drawn game and whose place was considered to be in jeopardy? What a good thing for Waterford that the selectors did not panic. Harney now knew (Tommy) O'Connell and that he had learned well the lessons of September 6th was proved on Sunday when O'Connell, a great hurler and regarded in Kilkenny as the re-incarnation of Mattie Power, was played into the ground until his very presence on the field went unnoticed. Could any man play a greater role in victory? Well, that was Joe Harney's role and how he played it.'

Joe was as solid as a rock and as dependable as they come.

He died on April 17, 2020.

AUSTIN FLYNN (FULL-BACK, ABBEYSIDE)

AUSTIN WAS AS hard as they come once he crossed that white line. He was an excellent full-back. And for all his achievements with Waterford, I think he was always disappointed that he never won a senior championship with Abbeyside. Austin was a great man for stories and he loved the sea… he always kept a boat.

One particular time he invited Philly Grimes up to Abbeyside for a spin out on the boat around Dungarvan Bay. Once they were out on the boat, Philly asked Austin if he could swim? Austin said he couldn't so Philly naturally asked what would happen if the boat went down.

'Sure, don't I play full-back. I'm used to hanging onto fellas… so I'll hang onto you!'

Unlike Philly, I never went out on the boat with Austin but we had many a long chat at different occasions over the years and when he started telling stories, you couldn't stop him. He talked as well as he hurled and he had a great knack for adding something to a story… I'd say he never told the same yarn in exactly the same way twice.

At Austin's funeral Mass, Fr Michael Enright, who'd sat in Croke Park with Austin for the 1954 All-Ireland football final, described Austin as 'a genius in his own right' and a gifted writer.

His grandson Gus, who hurls with Ballygunner, shared one of Austin's pearls of wisdom at the funeral:

'When things go wrong as they sometimes will, when the road you're trudging seems all uphill, when the funds are low and the debts are high, and you want to smile but you have to sigh, when care is pressing you down a bit, rest if you must but don't you quit.'

After Austin's passing, neighbours of his, Kieran (of WLR commentating fame) and Bernie O'Connor described him as 'a gentle giant' and 'the prince of full-backs'. That he surely was, on both counts.

A pure gentleman.

Austin died on April 26, 2021.

JOHN BARRON (CORNER-BACK, DE LA SALLE)

JOHN WAS SUCH a cool customer. Even though I played with him in the juvenile and Street Leagues and with Clover Meats, and friendly and all as we were, I don't think I ever really got to know him. And we had a geographical connection as well as the Pioneer magazine of 1959 pointed out:

His father, like Martin Morrissey's, is a native of Tullogher, a south Kilkenny parish which, strangely enough, is more concerned with football than hurling; that the fathers of two of the players on a team which so greatly enhanced Waterford's hurling prestige should come from a non-hurling area has not escaped the notice of those who are still discussing that wonderful game of September 6th.'

John was a very quiet fella. You wouldn't know he was around most of the time but my goodness, he really came to life every time he played Mount Sion. He didn't like Mount Sion at all and hurling us really brought the competitor out in him... and he often said that himself. I remember when we played De La Salle at Walsh Park in 1963 and a bit of a row developed between John and Frankie Walsh and they went on the knuckles.

The referee walked over and asked for both their names, which they volunteered.

'Head for the sideline now.'

I approached the referee, tapped him on the shoulder and said, 'Are you mad?' He replied: 'Why, what's wrong?'

'We're playing the National League final next Sunday... and you're going to send both of them off?' I informed him.

Well, in double quick time, knowing what the consequences might have been for Waterford, the ref repented and said to John and Frankie, 'Any more of that and I'll put you off'. The two lads played in the league final and the rest is history.

John also won four successive Railway Cup medals with Munster between 1958 and '61 and retired from inter-county hurling in '64.

He died on April 28, 2008.

MICK LACEY (WING-BACK, CAPPOQUIN)

BEING FROM THE west of the county, I didn't get to know Mick very well away from the hurling field. But he always had a pleasant way about him. He was a really good hurler and applied himself very well to the game.

Back in 1958, Tipperary trounced us in the Munster final by 4-12 to 1-5... not one of our better days during that era, let's face it. Before that match, we were approached by a certain individual whose name I'm not mentioning here, who said he was going to get us some 'pep' tablets. So he got them for us and we took them.

Well, not quite all of us.

Mick never took one. And everyone bar Mick Lacey played poorly in that Munster final. We always maintained afterwards that the fella who sourced these tablets had been supplied them by a Tipperary man! We'd been fed downers rather than uppers, we joked for years afterwards.

By the way, there were never any tablets or supplements used again afterwards. Once was once too many. If there'd been Man of the Match awards at the time, Mick would surely have got it.

A bit like John Mullane in the 2008 All-Ireland final, Mick was defiant when the rest of us didn't hurl anywhere close to our potential.

Mick worked hard on the basics and was a solid man to have alongside me in the half-back line.

He died in December 1997.

MARTIN ÓG MORRISSEY (CENTRE-BACK, MOUNT SION)

I STOOD AT less than five foot eight inches during my playing days and I was often playing against fellas who might be six foot two or three. I always tried to keep the ball out of their hands, so when a ball was dropping in from a puck-out or clearance from their back line… I'd be tapping the ball out in front of me.

I wouldn't be putting my hand up to catch it because I wouldn't have a prayer of fielding it against a taller man and, most of the time, I was marking someone taller. So my thing was to tap the ball out… then follow it and puck the ball down the field.

There was a chap who used to live up my way who worked with Mick Hayes, who had played for Waterford in 1948. He told me that when Mick was going to inter-county matches to watch us play, he'd say, 'All I'd want is a bottle in my hand, then I'd sit up on the bank and watch Óg batting them balls down and clearing them'.

That was my style of play.

Nowadays, the focus is all about getting the ball into the hand. The players might be moving faster today, what will all the improvements in training methods and physical training, but I still think the ball moved faster in my time than it does now. The matches in the 50s and 60s didn't lack for skill or good technique, but there was a more instinctive approach to the way we hurled then.

And I think we did alright for ourselves.

JACKIE CONDON (WING-BACK, ERIN'S OWN)

JACKIE WAS WHAT I'd describe as a 'tearaway' hurler. He was incredibly effective. I remember Philly Grimes saying to me that if we'd had Jackie Condon at wing half back in 1963 at Croke Park that we'd have won the All-Ireland final.

It was all the same to Jackie who he was marking or who came down his flank of the field... he was always ready and willing to have a go. He was a real case of 'the devil takes the hindmost' when it came to the opposition.

As a half-back line, I think there were different levels of understanding between the line I played in with Mount Sion compared to Waterford, and I can't for the life of me say why that was, even all these years later. I'm not saying that one was better or worse than the other, but they were most certainly different.

With Waterford, the idea of the three of us each sweeping at different times didn't really apply... you played your own position, although I was able to swing out behind Jackie and Mick and cover them. With Mount Sion from about the age of 14, we were advised to play a certain way, in a way I don't think necessarily applied with Erin's Own for Jackie or for Mick with Cappoquin... that the centre-half-back would cover the two wing half backs and vice-versa. But the three of us worked well together.

We were solid more often than not.

We did our job well.

SEAMUS POWER & PHILLY GRIMES
(MIDFIELD, BOTH MOUNT SION)

SEAMUS HAD A great understanding with Philly Grimes.

Raymond Smith, writing in *The Hurling Immortals* thought likewise. What a combination they were.

Seamus Power's inter-county career began in 1949, but it was in 1957 that he became a star. He started at left-wing in the All-Ireland final against Denis Heaslip – it was the first time he had ever played in the back-line – but after twenty minutes he switched to midfield. He became best known as a midfielder, though in 1965 he played in the full line of attack with Phil Grimes and Mick Flannelly.

The Seamus Power-Philly Grimes midfield partnership was, to my mind, as strong a pairing as has ever represented any county. Grimes brought style and class to everything he did on the hurling field. The Mount Sion man made a notable contribution to

Waterford's Munster championship win in 1948 and fifteen years later he was a match-winner against Tipperary in the National League (Home) final at Croke Park. Few could play John Doyle better.

Seamus was what I'd describe as an outstanding disruptor at centrefield, while Philly was, for me, the complete hurler. They complemented each other brilliantly and they were, without doubt, the best midfield pairing I ever had in front of me with Waterford. Seamus gave incredible service to Mount Sion, winning 16 senior championships in all – 12 for hurling and four for football. He went on to serve as a trainer and selector with club and county, became a respected inter-county referee and gave 14 years as club secretary before taking over the chairmanship after Pat Fanning was elected GAA President in 1970.

As Phil Fanning (Pat's son) wrote of Philly in the *Waterford News & Star* in February 2021:

He was a natural from a young age with his perfectly toned physique. He chose hurling and for him the hurley became part of himself through which he demonstrated the sheer artistry of his craft… my abiding memory from (the 1963 league final) is watching Philly Grimes taking off on a run along the Hogan Stand side towards the Railway end, ahead of a high clearance out of the Waterford defence, and while travelling at full speed catching the ball waist high in the palm of his hand behind him and without breaking stride going on to score a point.

It was almost as one would now see a wide receiver collecting from a quarterback at full speed only the ball was much smaller as was the palm of the hand.

Philly, the only Waterford hurler with four Munster senior winner's medals prior to 2010, is one of only two Déisemen to have featured in two victorious All-Ireland senior panels and claimed 18 senior championships (14 in hurling and four in football) with Mount Sion. They were both named in Waterford's Centenary Team in 1984 and the Millennium Team in 2000. It was an honour to know them and hurl with them.

Philly died on May 8, 1989… his 60th birthday.

Seamus died on June 25, 2016.

MICK FLANNELLY (WING-FORWARD, MOUNT SION)

POUND FOR POUND, Mick was as good a player as any I ever played with. Despite being smaller and lighter than nearly everyone else in every match he played in, you'd never get the end of Mick. In all the years I played with him, whether he was wing half-forward or wing half-back, I only ever saw one player get the better of him – a county final at Walsh Park against Abbeyside – and that was 'Duck' Whelan.

If you went to hit Mick with your body, he'd have the ball flicked onto someone else and then, more often than not, he'd dart out of the way and avoid the contact. Mick, who captained Waterford's All-Ireland minor winning team in 1948, was as clever as he was nimble. He recalled that success in an Irish Examiner interview in 2013.

'I wasn't a big man, and I was playing centre-forward on the minor team, but my father used to advise me, and he always said to spread the play, that you'd have the winning of the game that way. And that's how we played — there wasn't any barging through fellas, we moved the ball fast through the lines, and we had plenty of speed on the team. It suited us to move the ball, so we did.'

Mick had great game intelligence. He played senior with Waterford for 16 seasons and won 15 Senior Hurling Championship medals with Mount Sion, along with four senior football titles, which makes him the club's most successful ever player. It's a record that will never be broken, I reckon.

Mick, whose working life began as a printer with *The Munster Express*, died on September 11, 2021.

TOM CHEASTY (CENTRE-FORWARD, BALLYDUFF)

I REMEMBER BILLY Rackard saying he could never handle Cheasty. Now that was some compliment to Tom's ability. From what I can gather, when he was at home on the farm, bringing in the cows for milking, Tom had a hurley and ball with him the whole time, zig-zagging between the cattle on their way towards the milking parlour. He was fiercely committed to hurling and improving his game all the time.

When you were playing on Tom and if you were on his back and he caught the ball in his hand, he'd twirl, leave you standing and be gone behind you in what felt like the blink of an eye. To this day, I still don't know how Tom could do that.

I marked Tom a good few times at club level – even at minor level – and I'd try and leave a step or two between us so, when he gathered the ball, I'd created a little bit of space so that when he dropped the ball, that gave me the chance to flick the ball away. Frankie Walsh reckoned I hurled the ears off Tom whenever our paths crossed but it was an always a challenge to play on him.

Tom took a lot of punishment but he always stood up to it. And to think he was still hurling aged 50... I told him he was cracked!

Jim Irish, who played in the 1963 All-Ireland final with Tom, described him as 'the greatest centre forward I ever played with or saw in Waterford'. Tom, who is as revered in Portlaw as he is at his end of the parish in Ballyduff, died on August 10, 2007.

FRANKIE WALSH (WING-FORWARD, MOUNT SION, CAPTAIN)

WHAT A GREAT bit of stuff. Frankie stood on ceremony for no one. He could whip the ball brilliantly and pick it in a flash. We used to call him 'The Nettle' because if you went near him you got stung!

When a Munster team was being picked for the Railway Cup one particular year, the story goes that Mick Mackey proposed Frankie which prompted someone else in the room to comment, 'He's a small man'. To which Mackey replied, 'I know that... but he hurls big'.

Frankie didn't usually have to look to see where the posts were. He hurled on instinct. He picked the ball and hit it... I don't think there's anyone playing now who played the way Frankie did.

Delivering the graveside oration in Ballygunner following Frankie's funeral, Phil Fanning said:

'Frankie was a man whose great heart was out of proportion to his slight physical frame; a man of a generous, caring disposition, loyal and courageous, all traits that stood to him in life and that made him the hurler that he was... When Pat Fanning died (in 2010), Frankie Walsh was the unanimous choice to take over as Life President of Cumann Cnoc Síon. It was an honour Frankie did not take lightly and though his tenure was short, it was memorable, as was everything about Frankie Walsh.'

A Harty Cup winner in 1953 who would go on to win 13 senior hurling titles and four senior football championships with Mount Sion, Frankie was a good one and a fine captain in 1959. As Liam Cahill put it, Frankie was, 'a Mount Sion man to the marrow of his bone. Fear Chnoc Síon go smior.'

He died on December 28, 2012.

LARRY GUINAN (CORNER-FORWARD, MOUNT SION)

LARRY WAS A little terrier out on the field. You just couldn't contain him.

I remember playing Kilkenny in Walsh Park... it was a wet day and I was in the forward line, up alongside Larry, who was making his senior debut. A schmozzle broke out around the square and Jim 'Link' Walsh, Kilkenny's big full-back, ended up on his rear end.

Larry gave as good as he got... he never shirked from anything. He told Tomás McCarthy:

'(Link Walsh) must have been about 18 stone! On a little fella like me on a muddy day! I remember this ball coming down, a high ball, and I pulled on it and I must have knocked out a few of his teeth! He caught my hurley and threw it into the crowd and beat me with (his) hurley. I had a sore backside that night!'

Larry's greatest day in a Waterford jersey, and he has said so himself, was the 1959 Munster semi-final in Cork when we beat Tipperary by 9-3 to 3-4. It was 8-2 to no score at half-time and Michael O'Hehir, on radio, wasn't sure that score was correct when he read it out. That day, Larry scored three goals on John Doyle, 'a big brute of a fella'.

Larry went home happy. We all did.

Along with his inter-county honours and five Railway Cups, Larry won 12 senior championships with the club and featured in each of the nine in-a-row title wins. He also played with the Waterford senior football team for five years and in 1957, Larry was part of the team which famously defeated Kerry in the Munster Championship... or infamously if you're from Kerry!

TOM CUNNINGHAM: (FULL-FORWARD, DUNGARVAN)

'CUNN WAS A great servant to his club, taking a committee position aged 20, featuring on the All-Ireland winning Waterford minor (1948) and senior (1959) teams and was a Munster Council delegate from 1967 to '91.

He scored the winning point in the famous 1957 Munster Football Championship win over Kerry and had the distinction of playing in both senior Munster finals that year.

On and off the field, Cunn thought things out. He was a methodical man. With Waterford, Cunn started off in the full-back line and he wound up as corner-forward. Cunn was a fine hurler and a bit like Guinan, you'd never get the end of him. He knew exactly what he was going to do in advance of getting the ball… he played on the balls of his feet from one end of a game to the other. He left nothing to chance.

In 1959, not only did Cunn play his part in our All-Ireland win, but with Larry Guinan and Frankie Walsh as umpires, he refereed that year's Munster Senior Football final between Kerry and Cork in Killarney. A year later, he was in charge of the drawn All-Ireland Senior Football semi-final between Down and Offaly. And in 1961, he managed the Dungarvan minor footballers to a county championship.

To suggest he packed a lot in was a bit of an understatement. In GAA terms, he really was the whole package. A true Gael.

Tom died peacefully at University Hospital Waterford (UHW) on April 28, 2022 aged 91.

JOHN KIELY: (CORNER-FORWARD, DUNGARVAN)

JOHNNY WAS ANOTHER physically small man in our starting team – not that that held him back in any way – and he began his career at centrefield, which was where he made his name.

I often thought he deserved 'the nettle' nickname more than Frankie Walsh! John was such a good hurler and his shock of grey hair literally made him the standout player in the team.

Terry Dalton, one of our selectors that year, described John as 'a little rubber ball; he was as strong as an ox, a wonderful worker and a great hurler'.

Along with Philly Grimes, John received an All-Ireland winner's medal in 1948 having featured in that year's Munster Championship first round win over Clare. They both went on to claim a second Celtic Cross 11 years later, making them, to this day, members of the most exclusive club in Waterford hurling.

John contributed heavily during the 1959 championship, scoring 3-5 in total, including 2-2 against Cork in the Munster final and two points in the drawn All-Ireland final. He won two Railway Cup medals in 1952 and '57 and was a top class handballer.

John died on June 18, 2004.

MICHAEL O'CONNOR (SUBSTITUTE, CAPPOQUIN)

MICKEY WAS ONE of two subs used in the 1959 replay, coming on in place of Mick Lacey. An All-Ireland minor winner in 1948, Mickey was a beautiful hurler and he had a great turn of pace. I remember Paddy Greene, who trained Mount Sion in my time, saying he'd love to see Mickey hurling in the back line rather than as a forward and that eventually happened in 1957. Having contracted TB in 1957, Mickey was thrilled to be back involved in '59, as he told local radio when marking the golden jubilee year in 2009.

'I had played quite a lot of games in 1957 both in hurling and football and I put a lot of work and effort into it and I loved it so I was at the top of my ability from a hurling point of view anyway and I'd complete confidence in my ability at that stage. But unfortunately, after '57, I was told by my doctor that I'd have to take it easy for five or six months, so I spent five months in hospital.

'I didn't get out until March 1958 so hurling was very secondary on my mind at that stage – I had other problems but I was lucky that I recovered quickly enough. I started, against all the advice, to hurl a little bit again so at the end of '58 I started to play the odd match locally with Cappoquin and I decided I'd have another effort at it in '59… I was on the panel and I didn't play during the campaign.

'I only came on as a sub in the All-Ireland and believe it or not, I suppose, as an act of appreciation, I was picked as a selector with the 1959 team and that kept me very involved as well.'

Mickey was an excellent man to have alongside me… he'd cover in behind and had a great positional sense.

Talk about a good skin.

DONAL 'DUCK' WHELAN (SUBSTITUTE, ABBEYSIDE)

'DUCK, WHO REPLACED Tom Cunningham in the replay, having started the drawn match, was a fairly big man and he used his strength a lot.

Duck was a nice character and a very effective full-forward.

CHARLIE WARE (ERIN'S OWN)

ANOTHER MAN WHO was replaced from the drawn match, with Mick Flannelly coming in for him. Charlie's own father – also called Charlie – hurled in the 1938 All-Ireland final defeat to Dublin, while his uncle Jim had the great honour of captaining the senior team against the same county when Waterford won its first MacCarthy Cup in 1948.

Charlie died on November 24, 2013.

SEVENTEEN OF US got to start between the drawn match and the replay in 1959 and we all made our contribution. Freddie O'Brien (Mount Sion), Paudie Casey (Ballygunner) and Joe Coady (Erin's Own) were the three non-playing subs for the replay.

Joe died on August 5, 2008.

WLR's KEVIN CASEY, Lord have mercy on him, interviewed myself and a good few more of the lads from 1959 to mark the 50th anniversary of our All-Ireland win. And a few of us rightly acknowledged the role that Pat Fanning (Mount Sion) played as county board chairman during that period. I told Kevin the following:

'Before Pat came in as chairman, when you'd go off playing a match, you'd maybe go in for a fish and chips, and get your bit of grub in, but the very minute Pat was made chairman, we were off to a hotel and that was it. You got the best.

'Talking about that too, Cork there a couple of years ago, one of the things they went on strike about was a doctor. We'd a doctor in 1957… Dr Shelley, you could go up to him any time you liked and he was at nearly every match we played. He wasn't being paid or anything like that but he was mad about the game.'

Pat died on March 14, 2010. He gave a lifetime of service to Mount Sion and Waterford. And between Pat and John Keane (Mount Sion), we knew we were in the best of hands at the time. As Seamus Power put it, 'They personified what Mount Sion meant and still means!'

John Keane was a huge figure in both club and county terms. He did it all both on and off the field and it's only right that he's held in as much regard as Waterford as Christy Ring is in Cork. He hurled in the 1938 and '48 All-Ireland finals and then trained us in '59… and that's only a fraction of his legacy. In David Smith's marvellous book about John, titled *The Unconquerable Keane*, Austin Flynn gave a great insight into John's instincts when it came to training us in the build-up to the All-Ireland final replay:

'The field in Waterford was having some work done on it and we were training in Dunhill. One night I was really enjoying the training and felt on top of the world when John abruptly stopped the session and said, "All right, lads, you've all done enough. Go in

and have a rub-down". Some of us were a bit annoyed but we did what we were told.

'It was only after we had won the All-Ireland that it struck us that John knew we had done enough training and that he didn't want us to leave all our hurling on the training pitch. We were super-fit and he knew any more training would have made us stale.'

John died on October 1, 1975. He was only 58.

Though we knew he'd been ill for quite some time, it was still a terrible shock when the news broke. He was on his way to see Mick Mackey that morning when he felt unwell on the road between Limerick and Tarbert. He knocked on a door and asked the woman who answered it to ring for an ambulance. He died in the ambulance before it reached Limerick.

John had visited many of his old comrades from his playing days just before he died – Jimmy Langton in Kilkenny, Jack Barrett below in Kinsale, Limerick's Jackie Power, who was living in Tralee by then – and Mackey was to have been his next port of call.

But he never made it.

I was proud to be one of John's pallbearers along with a host of fellow clubmen… Paddy Greene, Frankie Walsh, Mick Healy, Larry Fanning, Andy Fleming, Larry Guinan, Mick Flannelly, Pat O'Grady, John Flynn, Philly Grimes, Séamus Power, Pat McGrath, Jim Greene, Dickie Roche and Davy Power. It was surely the only time any of us ever carried John Keane, who was laid to rest in Tramore.

Delivering the graveside oration, Pat Fanning said:

'He has gone from us but lives on in our hearts, and his family can be assured that while hurling is played, his name will be remembered and the young hurlers of tomorrow will seek to recapture the spirit and emulate the deeds of a man who for so long bestrode the hurling scene like a colossus…John Keane of Mount Sion.

'God rest you, John Keane.

'You were a good one.'

That he surely was.

IT WAS VERY satisfying the way it all came together in 1959 and it was a feather in our cap to beat Kilkenny in an All-Ireland final. Not only that, but we beat Galway, Cork, Tipperary and Kilkenny to win the MacCarthy Cup and the significance of beating four of the biggest traditional hurling counties didn't dawn on us straightaway.

It was the equivalent of Ireland winning the Grand Slam in rugby and we were the first team to beat those four teams to win an All-Ireland senior title.

Mind you, I still think a lot of us should have ended up with three All-Ireland winners' medals. But we had a good team. A very good team, even. We played fast, open hurling and that earned us great admiration all over the country.

The Waterford team who were Kings of Ireland in 1959, and Martin Óg is carried high from the winning field in Croke Park.

« CHAPTER 9 »

In the Trenches with Óg

I HAD THE good fortune to play with a host of great players, with the Mount Sion school and then the club, on Railway Cup duty with Munster and, of course, more than a few in the white and blue of Waterford. Larry Guinan and Michael O'Connor were among them and we're still the right side up, kept going by our families, good company and many a well-spun yarn from those great days when we played 60 or more years ago.

◄◄◆►►

Larry Guinan

'ÓG ALWAYS HAD a good idea of just how useful a hurler he was.

'One day stands out in my mind when I think about him. We were in Limerick after playing Tipperary and they gave us an awful beating. Well, we were on our way home that evening and we stopped in Clonmel for fish and chips.

'Óg and myself were walking away from the chip shop and who did we meet only his two sisters Bridie and Maura. They threw their arms around Martin Óg and said to him, "What harm, Martin Óg, it wasn't your fault!"

'I was the only other witness to this at the time but I've never forgotten it.

But my goodness, he was an excellent player. I knew it, his sisters knew it and, of course, the man himself knew that too.

'I remember coming onto the Waterford team and looking up to the likes of Óg, Seamus Power and Philly Grimes… they were all older than me and well established in the senior team by the time I got the nod. Those men were gods to me. I never thought I'd end up playing in the same team as them and it was a great honour for me to play with them.

'I was captain of Waterford in 1962 when we won the Oireachtas, and that was a very prestigious competition at the time. Winning that and the league the following year meant we completed the set when it came to the main hurling competitions and it was a huge honour for me to be the man collecting the cup in Croke Park after beating Tipperary by six points.

'But as legend has told it since, and by legend I mean Martin Óg, it wasn't Waterford who beat Tipp that day, it was Óg… and that's the story he has stuck to for the past 60 years, so I can't see him changing his tune now! But I do mean this sincerely… I've always been sorry I was the one who accepted the cup after that match.

'It should have been Óg because it really was *his* day. He was outstanding that day. I mean he was always a very consistent and reliable performer but that particular day he was phenomenal. No matter what came his way, he dealt with it.

'He could be a lazy so-and-so at times but he was certainly moving that day. He was brilliant. It was the best game I ever saw him play.

'Óg had fierce strength and his pull on the ball off the ground was something else. I've often said it to the lads here in the (tyre) shop over the years that he could cut a ball off the ground and drive it 70 yards. If he was hitting a ball today from the half-back line, with the ball they're using now, he'd put it over the bar.

'Martin Óg and Theo English of Tipperary (1930-2021) were the two best men I ever saw cutting a ball. He had unreal power and he put it to good use for the club and the county. He was something else.

'Óg was always his own man. He'd great respect for the men training us, Paddy Greene most of all, I'd say, but he knew his mind and no-one expected more of himself in a match than Óg himself. He was always uptight before matches, and you wouldn't get too many words out of him in the minutes before we'd head out of the dressing-room, but I think that was mainly down to his level of concentration and getting his head clear for the next hour or so.

'And then, he'd go out and do his job as well as anyone I can think of ever did at centre-half-back during my playing days. He rarely let himself down, or anyone else down once he crossed that white line. Funnily enough, another thing that comes to mind is Óg having pigeons in the back of the car and then leaving them out in places like Kilkenny, Thurles and so on.

'I think he always had an interest in them. Óg was always a good teammate and a funny fella. And he was a very good looking fella. He used to compare himself to the film actor Jeff Chandler …and after Óg got a scar on his face he said he looked even more like Chandler after that.

'He was a fine man, no two ways about it.

'GOOD AND ALL as the health has been to me over the years, thank God, once enough years have passed, it's hard enough to recall too many specific things from those matches that mightn't have attracted the headlines the way Munster and All-Ireland finals did in our time and still do today.

'The day I got the nod for Waterford, early in 1957, is still pretty clear in the mind, though. I was at home in Árd na Gréine the day Waterford were playing Kilkenny in the National League when there was a knock on the door around midday, and who was it only Pat Fanning.

'And Pat said to me, "Will you play for Waterford today?"

'What?' was my immediate reply.

'I don't think I really took in what Pat was saying to me straightaway.

' "Will you play for Waterford today?" he repeated. So I did and that was the start of 16 years of senior hurling with the county.

'The penny dropped with me… I said "Yes", gathered up my gear and made the short walk to Walsh Park. It was totally out of the blue, so up I went… I played and where did they put me only in at full-forward. A little bit of a fella like me at full-forward, going up against about 18 stones weight of the 'Link' Walsh.

'I doubt if a man that big has ever played at full-back for any county since then. Talk about a baptism of fire. They absolutely hammered us yet we still ended up in the All-Ireland final that same year and we were only beaten by a point by Kilkenny. And that's definitely a game we should have won.

'We were definitely more heavily backed to win the 1963 final than we were the '57 final. You have to remember we were after winning the Oireachtas in 1962, and we followed that up by winning the league and the Munster Championship, so we were on course for the clean sweep of all senior trophies for the very first time but, unfortunately, as was the case in 1957, Kilkenny got the better of us in the '63 final as well.

'That 1957 defeat was a very hard one to take. I remember us being five or six points clear at one stage when Seamus Power had a ball out on the sideline and he hit it in towards goal and nothing came of it. For years after that, he'd say to me he should have "dawdled" a bit over it and been a bit cleverer with the ball than he was, but it wasn't as if that was the reason we lost, at least it wasn't as far as I was concerned.

'It just got away from us that day and I'd maintain we were unlucky. Losing by a point is always a sickener. Winning is within your grasp… only to lose out by the finest of margins. You'd sooner lose a game by 10 points than by one. It's easier to deal with when you lose a game when there's a bit of a gap.

'Whenever you lose by a point, you come off the field knowing that if just one thing had gone the other way, we'd have either had a replay or we'd have won. That was a very hard one to take. And to think Mick Kenny scored a point for Kilkenny that day when he was on his knees. Give him that ball nine other times and he'd probably not have scored… but off his knees, striking a heavy ball… he stuck it over the bar.

'A year later, we were on the end of a heavy defeat to Tipperary. No round robin, no back door, we were out of the Championship before we knew it. Tipp went onto win the All-Ireland, beating Galway in the final, not that that mattered too much to us in hindsight. After coming so close to winning the All-Ireland the previous year…to be beaten so heavily in the following Munster final was a huge disappointment. We knew we were a lot better than that.

Now, we played Kerry in the first round in 1958 and I remember us tossing a ball around in an old field all the way out in Kenmare and we were nearly blaggarding more than we were warming up. We thought the whistle would blow, the ball would be thrown in and we'd beat Kerry, no problem. But it didn't turn out that way at all.

'We beat them in the end by 3-9 to 2-4 but we were never comfortable at any stage in that game. Then Tipp slaughtered us. God, that was a poor year for us but thankfully we got our wits about us when it came to 1959 and we did what we should have done in '57, even if it took a second day to get to the job done… we finally beat Kilkenny in an All-Ireland final.

'Years later, when I had a filling station on the Cork Road in Waterford, myself, Tom Cheasty and Philly Grimes were having a chat about hurling – what else? – when Grimesey took off, showing how fit he was. He cleared a high wall like an Olympic hurdler. He was an incredible athlete.

'Another day, he appeared with a skipping rope and made it sing. Ah, Philly was exceptional… he could have thrown his hat at any number of sports and excelled at them all. And in today's game, with such an emphasis on strength, nutrition and so on, Philly would have made the cut. He was *exceptional*.

'And everyone who played with him, and I'd say nearly everyone he ever played against, admired him. We'd some brilliant men on that team but Philly was just exceptional.

'IN 1959, WE bamboozled Tipperary in the Munster semi-final. We were bursting with confidence that day. We just exploded out of the blocks and Tipp didn't know what hit them. They were the defending champions and we swept the floor with them.

'I scored three goals that day so that was a very special one for me, understandably. Three goals against the All-Ireland holders… days like that don't come around too often. We just ate them without salt… we were bursting with confidence. Everything we were capable of producing as a team came out of us that day.

'I remember Frankie Walsh crossing an amazing ball into me from one side of the field to the other and all I had to do was bat it into the net. It was a truly great team to be part of and to pick off Galway, Cork, Tipperary and Kilkenny the way we did… to score 23 goals across those five matches, it really was one for the ages.

'We probably should have won the first day out against Kilkenny but when the full-time whistle went, Frankie was convinced we had lost by a point. He picked up a bottle in the dressing-room and he smashed it against the wall, that's how annoyed he was. But once he was told we were after drawing and that we'd another chance to win, that calmed him down and put him in a better frame of mind.

'Looking back, I reckon we were lucky to draw the first day even thought I still thought we were the better team. We had our second chance and we took it. That was probably as comfortable a win as any of us could ever have imagined in an All-Ireland final.

'We were confident going into that game.

'We felt there was more in us than we'd shown in the drawn game and it panned out that way, thankfully. As happy as we were, there was definitely a feeling of relief as well, in that we'd proven that we could not only compete with the best, but that we could beat them all. We well and truly earned that All-Ireland title.

'That weekend could have been notable for a few other things that thankfully didn't happen. We went swimming at four o'clock the following morning and both Seamus Power and 'Duck' Whelan nearly drowned… they went out beyond their depth and got into some trouble.

'Thankfully, things worked out in the end. On our way home to Waterford, we took a corner somewhere near Ballyhale and there was a local car coming towards us and we came within inches of a crash. The man driving the car ended up in the ditch but, thank God, he came out of it in one piece.

'Any time Waterford beat Kilkenny in hurling is a special occasion so to beat them in an All-Ireland final really was as good as it could get for us. Beating Tipperary was special but in a different way as far as I was concerned.

'An uncle of mine, Tom Gough, hurled for Tipp… and he'd a grandson, Oisín, who won an All-Ireland club medal with Cuala, so there's no doubting the breeding there! But beating Kilkenny was definitely the ultimate and at least it's something the senior team has started doing again over the last few years.

'I always mixed well with all the lads on our panel. They were an incredibly decent bunch and made for great company. I idolised John Kiely. He was my best friend when I played in the corner and he was full-forward. Austin Flynn was one of the best friends I ever had and Mickey O'Connor is still going great guns at over 90 years of age.

'The way he recovered from TB after being in Ardkeen for months and got back into the panel tells you all you need to know about what kind of man Mickey is.

'OUR LAST HURRAH at the highest level was the 1963 All-Ireland final and that's another match, nearly 60 years later, that still sticks in the craw.

'We were hot favourites that day, probably the first time any Waterford team went into an All-Ireland as favourites… we scored six goals, yet we still lost. Eddie Keher scored heavily that day and a lot of his scores came from frees. I coughed up two frees to Keher and then he went in on Óg and he got a bit of change out of Óg as well… yet he wasn't Man of the Match.

'I ended up going into full-forward towards the end of the game – I was mainly operating at half-back at the time – but I scored nothing after I was switched. I'd be in the forward line one year, then the back line the following year and I did find moving around like that quite unsettling. I loved playing at corner-forward and between 1957 and '59, in both the league and championship, I was first to score for us in most games.

'But then they started shoving me into the backline and what with me being so keen to play, I just got on with it. You did what you were told, and that was it. The same went for Óg and everyone else on the team. High standards were demanded of us and we did our best to keep our levels high.

'There was one evening at training when John Keane gave us an instruction… no one was to handle the ball. I was young enough at that stage. I was out on the field, hitting the ball along the ground the whole time and then this one ball hopped in front of me and I caught it.

'And boy, did Keane give it to me.

'He reddened me, so much so that I shed tears that day. I had wicked respect for John Keane, we all did and we never wanted to let him down. But I got over that quickly enough, even though I've never forgotten it.

'Óg, myself and a good few more of the club were pallbearers at John's funeral. He went far too young.

'We had one more Munster final beyond 1963… the 1966 final against Cork in Limerick which we lost by two goals (4-9 to 2-9) and I scored one of ours. Not too long ago, I got a letter from a chap called Tony Connolly who played for Cork in that final and he sent me on a photo which Annie Brophy, a very well-known photographer in Waterford for years, took of Frankie Walsh and myself in our Waterford kits and all the trophies we won between the club and county in 1959.

'It was originally taken in black and white and then someone made a colour version of it which got published in the *Examiner*. Now I'd seen it before, but to think after all these years that Tony put that in the post to me, that says a lot. We'd great respect for each other and it's nice to be remembered all these years later.

'And just as Tipp did in '58 after beating us in the Munster final, Cork went all the way in 1966, beating Kilkenny in the All-Ireland. By 1966, I think only Tom Cheasty and myself were left from '57. And it's hard to believe we haven't won an All-Ireland since then... we could have almost sneaked one in 1998 and if we'd won that one, I'd say we'd have added a few in the meantime.

'But every team we've had since 1963 has tended to have a bit of a tail... in fact, you could argue we were even short one or two in our own time, be it on the starting team or on the line. The 2017 final against Galway had more than a touch of '57 about it... that's a match we could definitely have won. I don't see that Galway team as having been all that superior to our team that day. Is it more a mental thing than an ability thing?

'Sure if any of us knew the answer to that, we'd be after winning a fair few All-Irelands since 1959.

'BY THE STANDARDS of the current era, especially when you take the size of most inter-county teams now, I don't think my Waterford team would be at the races. We'd be too small... Grimesey and Austin were the only two players we had you might describe as tall. We're bits of men in comparison to the big athletes hurling nowadays.

'But I realise we're not comparing like with like either. It was a different game in our time and it was played in a different way... sure it's a different game now than it was 20 years ago. It'd be great to see ground hurling coming back. There's far too much 'arseing' around for my liking nowadays and the clash of the ash is gone from hurling now, even though it's a faster game which I still find lovely to watch.

'We got nothing easy in our time.

'We enjoyed our successes between the All-Ireland, the three Munster titles, the league... and the Oireachtas Óg won for us, but we should have won more than one All-Ireland title. And while we were very lucky to win that one All-Ireland and while we were very happy about it, we know we should have won more than we did.

'But it really is time to bury it now.

'God almighty, I'd do anything to see a Waterford man climb the steps of the Hogan Stand and lift the MacCarthy Cup before all of us from 1959 are gone.

There's not too many of us left, we're drifting away but I pray to God, while we're alive, that Waterford can do it.'

◄◄◆►►

MICHAEL O'CONNOR GAVE a great interview to none other than his brother Kieran on WLR which went out in January 2022. He was good enough to give me a reference when he looked back on his time in the Waterford jersey and given what he went through with his health prior to 1959, he earned that Celtic Cross more than the rest of us did.

◄◄◆►►

Michael O'Connor

'I WAS FORTUNATE to play with many excellent players but, for me, Phil Grimes was my outstanding player on the Waterford team. He was a fine athlete but he was also a beautiful hurler and striker of the ball. He had everything you'd want (in a player) so he would be my number one.

'Another very good player that I have to mention was our centre half-back, Martin Óg Morrissey, who was an exceptional striker of the ball and I played with Martin Óg in the half-back line for years…

'Training with the Mount Sion and Erin's Own, players definitely improved the players from the rest of the county. They were friendly and we felt welcome down there. We were looked on as part of a team and that was it.

'John Keane was a very quiet gentleman and he knew the hurling inside out. He had his own quiet way of getting things done and I think he succeeded. We'd a very fast team and we played a lot of ground hurling which you don't see nowadays, and if we got a nice pitch with fast ground, we knew we'd be very hard to beat.

'When it came to training… I always loved it. I never drank and I never smoked so all that stood to me.

'I HAD A very good year in 1957.

'Cappoquin beat Mount Sion in the Sargent Cup final on our pitch, Waterford won the Munster Championship and reached the All-Ireland final… and I was selected for Munster's Railway Cup team. That was probably my biggest boost, being picked for Munster.

'During the winter, I used to be interested in all sporting activities but particularly foxhunting that I used to enjoy of a Sunday with the Dungarvan Harriers, so when I was picked for Munster I decided to get rid of the horse and concentrated on hurling and that really was the boost I needed.

'We played Leinster in the final. Christy Ring was our captain and while there were a lot of big names in the dressing-room, I didn't feel overawed. I'd a lot of confidence in my own ability. I knew I had a lot of speed. I was 27 at that stage and I was confident in terms of what I could do. In the final, I marked Tim Flood of Wexford and he was a beautiful hurler, one of the fairest men you could be marking. There was no dirty stroke in him… he was a very clean player.

'I remember Mick Mackey was a (Munster) selector and I went for the first ball with Tim Flood and I just blocked… I didn't pull and I was trying to read Tim and size him up a bit, to see just how good he was. Mackey turned to the Waterford selector and he said, "I don't know about this fella".

'So the next ball came anyway and I'd my mind made up about what I was going to do, so I pulled hard on the ball, gathered it and cleared it. Then Mackey turned back to the same selector and said, "Oh yes, he'll be alright".

'Winning the Railway Cup was a huge thing for me and a great honour. As for playing with Christy Ring? Well, there was no comparison in hurling terms with him. He was so fast, such a wonderful striker of the ball and his wristwork. He was a true specialist…

'In 1958, TB struck. I remember Dr Alfie O'Donovan calling into the old (Cappoquin Chickens) factory to have a word with me. He said, "Look, you went for an x-ray in July or August and I think they want to repeat it so you'd better go and have it checked out". So I checked it out alright and I ended up *having my holidays* in Ardkeen (Hospital) for five months after that.

'I found that time very hard but I decided that I'd better try and fight this thing and do what I'm told down in Ardkeen… take my medicines and take my rest. And thankfully, after five months, I was all clear and at the end of it all I was told I was fine and that I could go home.

'All the time I was down there, I was fairly determined to get back playing hurling and I felt stronger than ever after it all. So I went back playing with Cappoquin and felt quite good and strong. I was made a selector for the Waterford team in 1959 but I was also put on the panel. Yet I resisted playing the whole time in that championship.

'I kept saying, "Ah, leave me alone" but they kept at me and at me, and I eventually and fortunately went on in the final, coming on as a substitute.

'To have myself and fellow clubman Mick Lacey involved in that final was a great honour for the town and we took a lot of pride in our Cappoquin jerseys. When we played for Cappoquin, we gave 100 percent. After 1959 and after I got married, by which time I was 30 years of age, my father had a quite substantial business in Cappoquin so I decided to put more effort into the business and I decided I wouldn't continue with inter-county hurling, so I packed it in.

'And I was fine with that decision. I was quite happy to have achieved what I achieved… you're gone over the top at 30…

'There's not many of us left from the 1959 group and it's always been hard to say goodbye to the men gone before us, but it's extraordinary how you maintain the friendship even though we mightn't meet that often.

'But we always looked on each other as friends… Martin Óg Morrissey, Frankie Walsh and Mick Flannelly, they were all really close friends of mine.'

◄◄◆►►

PAT FANNING WAS always a great man for a few words before the ball was thrown in. He was as obsessed with hurling, and with Mount Sion and Waterford's success as anyone before him or since. Towards the end of 2008, he was interviewed as part of the GAA's Oral History project. Pat was 90 years old at the time and his interest in the game was as strong as ever.

◄◄◆►►

Pat Fanning

'THE 1955-63 TEAM was one of the finest teams any county ever produced and I put it to them (in 1955) that we should be sick of being patronised and that we should realise that we had the ability and that we had the will to do great things.

'And the story of 1955 to '63 is a demonstration of what the will to win, coupled with ability, can achieve in the county…

'This is something I'm very, *very* proud of and will preach as long as I'm left here on this earth… and that is that ours is a tradition in hurling as proud and as much to talk about as that of Tipperary or Cork or Kilkenny or the great hurling counties because ours is a tradition of continuing effort, where the clubs are strong, where the clubs are pledged to the association and where the county has never ceased in its straining for success.'

◄◄◆►►

YES, WE SHOULD have won more than one All-Ireland title.

To win that one meant a lot to us and still does today.

But… it's high time we won a third MacCarthy Cup.

The social life attached to the game during the 1950s and 60s made the playing of gaelic games far more rewarding than it is today. And (below) Martin Óg pictured with Paddy 'Moremiles' Murphy and Frankie Walsh.

« CHAPTER 10 »

Training and Succeeding...
on Both Sides of the Suir

The man with the Midas touch in the Glenmore camp must surely be trainer, Martin Óg Morrissey. He has now completed a magnificent treble of junior, intermediate and senior championship successes with the Southerners. In 1985, he was in the other camp, and trained Shamrocks to their senior win over Glenmore. What is their secret? 'Dedication, that is what it is all about,' he said. 'There is no big secret. If you don't get a response from the players you can't do anything. These Glenmore players were very, very dedicated."

– The Kilkenny People, November 6, 1987

AS THE YEARS passed by, I did make time for pursuits outside of my family, work and hurling. Jackie White, my brother-in-law was big into shooting... it was something he'd done since childhood thanks to his father, who having been born and bred out in the countryside, was hugely into it himself.

So, just out of pig iron I went out with Jackie once or twice just to see what I made of it and I took a shine to it. This was just around the time I was winding up as a player with Mount Sion when I turned 40. Now, I'd started giving a bit of time to training teams by then and that was mostly on Sunday evenings to begin with.

If you never shot a bird – be it pheasant, snipe or woodcock – you were still getting plenty of exercise so there was something to take out of it before you'd even loaded a barrel. I don't think it was a case of me looking for something to replace playing, but at the same time I grew very fond of it and had many a good day out thanks to it.

And ultimately, training teams was almost as time intensive as things were for me while I was playing.

My high point with shooting wasn't the shooting at all… it was watching the dogs working. Over time I realised that having a good dog with you was more important than whatever you shot. We went to any number of places shooting… mostly over the river in Slieverue, Mullinavat, Ballyhale and in Tullogher, and I only gave it up in my early to mid-eighties.

Frank, our second son, took up shooting and we used to head off together with Sean Grace from Piltown and it was very enjoyable. It wasn't something too many people in the city would have entertained themselves with, but it was a good old past time… you'd be gone at daybreak and you wouldn't come back 'til dinner time and you might go off then again after dinner as well. In total, you could be out strolling with a few fellas and the dogs for anything between six and eight hours, and I got a lot out of it.

I do remember one frosty morning going up the river with Jackie and John Heffernan – another brother-in-law of mine who lived in Cheekpoint, the Lord have mercy on him – and we went out to shoot duck. I was nearly stuck to the boat with the cold given how thick a coat of frost was on the ground that morning.

When we came in, I said to John, 'That is my last f***ing duck shoot… I'm not going to shoot duck anymore.' Sitting in the boat, in the cold of an early morning with my fingers going blue wasn't my idea of fun, so I didn't go back out in the boat for that purpose again after that.

I shot plenty of birds over the years… God knows, I missed my fair share too. Now that I don't shoot, of course I miss it. I miss it a lot. But a bit like my playing days, it was good while it lasted.

But to go back almost 50 years, hurling still had me firmly in its grip and as much as I loved going to Waterford matches with my good friend Paddy Murphy, training teams felt like a natural progression for me. I'd more in my head about hurling at 40 than I did at 20 or 30, so why let it go to waste?

THE FIRST GROUP I had for training were the under-21s at Mount Sion, who won the county championship, including Eamon Ryan and Pat McGrath who progressed all the way to senior, along with Tommy Cusack and Geoff Keogh, who were such reliable performers for us. Good lads the lot of them.

It was very satisfying to see lads like the two Pats progressing the way they did and doing their bit to keep the game and the club going.

I'd a fairly simple philosophy, and the truth be told I don't even know if I'd describe it as a philosophy, but I insisted on players doing what they were told at training and during a match. When it came to training, I took my cues from Paddy Greene's approach during my own playing days when he was training us… a match every night at training, and I feel that stood to the players.

We were carrying on a tradition Paddy had established, a tradition that brought huge success to Mount Sion so I saw little point in trying to write a completely new training manual. I enjoyed training. At times I might have lost my cool with fellas acting the mick during training sessions but, to be fair, the lads were great.

Sure look at all they won?

And when it came to matches, with Seamus Power, Jimmy Morrissey, 'Fluff' Fanning and Dickie Roche on the line alongside me at different times, I was in some company. We were always pretty cool during matches. I suppose we were fortunate to be looking after players who were winning so regularly and that gave them and us in turn a good deal of confidence.

After the 14s, I was involved with the under-16s, the under-21s and the senior team, and we ended up winning a couple of under-21 (1973 and '74) and senior championships. We beat Portlaw in the 1975 final by 6-4 to 2-7 in a replay at Walsh Park… played with the wind and had three goals scored inside six minutes.

And while Portlaw never threw the towel in, they had too much ground to make up as we won our 24th senior championship. In 1975, the players gave us everything. That was an excellent side. Jim Greene – Paddy's son – was one of the stars in that team and would go on to win an All Star with Waterford in 1982.

I've known Jim since he was a young fella and we've been lifelong friends. And when we're in each other's company, hurling is always on the tip of both our tongues.

◄ ◄ ◆ ► ►

Jim Greene

'ÓG WAS A great tactician, an extremely good hurling coach and a perfectionist in his own way. He didn't like mediocrity so he was never cut out to be a good man manager. He was better suited to being a selector and a trainer, as he was with Mount Sion and Waterford and he was great in that role.

'It suited him down to a tee. In 1982, the year I won my All Star and I was 33 by then, we reached the Munster final and were beaten badly by Cork in Thurles (5-31 to 3-6). No one came near us after it.

'That day in Semple Stadium was worse for me than the day my father died. It was that painful. Now someone might wonder how could losing a hurling match be worse than the day my father died, but he was a very sick man so when he died, there was an element of relief to it for his sake. Anyone who has seen someone suffer for a considerable period will have some idea about the point I'm making here… because it was worse and worse the poor man was getting and it was a Godsend that he was taken.

'I felt so bad after that Munster final. It was so unreal to be beaten like that in front of 45,000 people… just wanting the ground to open up and swallow you.

'Going back and hurling with our clubs was the antidote to that day in Thurles.. but nobody in the county board contacted any of us after that loss to Cork. The press we got, how we felt about it as a group of players afterwards… it was a complete horror story.

'It was a far cry from the sports psychology of the modern inter-county game.

'As players, we realised we only had each other.

'A meeting was called up in a hotel in Ballyrafter, just outside Lismore, because at the time we felt that something needed to change. We weren't happy with things… now maybe it was all our fault, but we felt that we – players and board members alike – should all be taking the post-Munster final punishment together because up to that meeting, no one in the board had come near us.

'The inference, to us anyway, was clear. So Pat Curran and myself, representing the players, went to the meeting and then we were told by the chairman John A

Murphy that we couldn't speak because we weren't a body. So, according to some protocol, the Waterford players were, officially, nobodies.

'The meeting reacted to that and called it for what it was… bull****, especially those representing the western clubs. "We're saying that Jim Greene and Pat Curran can't talk at the meeting? Sure that's nonsense". Well that protocol was knocked on the head there and then, so both Pat and I were permitted to speak after all.

'So I took to the floor and said my piece and the selectors were changed… we had looked for Óg for 1983 and we got him. Now that didn't last very long because, I think, we as players put him in there.'

◄◄◆►►

I'D BEEN TRAINER with the Waterford under-21s that reached the 1974 All-Ireland hurling final, the only All-Ireland any Waterford team reached at any grade during the 70s. You'd the likes of John Galvin, Pat McGrath, Tom Casey, Kieran Ryan and Liam O'Brien in that group and they were a very good panel to train.

We lost that final by a single point to Kilkenny (3-8 to 3-7) and it could have gone either way. But those players never kicked on the way they'd have wanted to with Waterford at senior level and while they reached the 1982 and '83 Munster finals, both ended in very heavy defeats to Cork… two days not fondly remembered in the county.

◄◄◆►►

Frank Morrissey

'I WAS THE Waterford under-21 ball-boy in 1974 for all their training sessions in Walsh Park. I was 12 years old. Maureen Quann and Johnny would have stacks of sandwiches and pints of milk ready for the players after training and matches there, and at that time I wouldn't eat butter. So Maureen, who was related to my mother, would always have sandwiches with no butter on them made especially for me. You should see the amount of butter I use now!

'When Waterford won the Munster under-21 title, Pat McGrath was awarded the cup but Eamonn Ryan was actually the captain… it was his turn to be captain, but Pat was told to go up and get the cup. So he came down out of the stand in Thurles and said, "Here, Frank, will you mind this!"... and he handed me the cup.

'So they all went off to the pub and there was me after them, wandering down to Liberty Square with the cup, wondering which pub they were all after going into!

'I'd been at the 1973 All-Ireland final with dad when Limerick beat Kilkenny, and I was crying coming home on the train after Kilkenny had lost. And I was at the 1974 final when Kilkenny won, getting the better of Limerick that time, and I was as happy as Larry. But when it came to the under-21 All-Ireland final that same year, I'd eyes only for Waterford... but Kilkenny had a good few lads from their senior team who were still eligible to play under-21, including Ger Fennelly, Billy Fitzpatrick and Brian Cody.

'They'd a really strong team, but Waterford definitely had the beating of Kilkenny that day... yet we lost by a point. And that ended up being our best chance at a major success in the whole of the 70s. John Galvin didn't benefit from some free-taking advice that day, unfortunately – not from my father, mind you – and it wasn't John's fault whatsoever.

'Beating Kilkenny in any way, shape or form is all that matters but we only seemed to have seen the wisdom of that over the last few years.

'My only year's involvement as a trainer with the Waterford senior panel was in 1983... Mick Flannelly and 'Duck' Whelan were two of the selectors also drafted in at the start of that year. We beat Tipperary in the Munster semi-final by 4-13 to 2-15 to reach a second successive Munster final, where Cork, who'd doled out a heavy beating to us in '82, were waiting once again. But for the second year in-a-row, we came home licking our wounds after a heavy defeat (3-22 to 0-12)... another hard day for us all to put down.

'The attitude of the players in both league and championship had been good, that was never in doubt as far as I was concerned, but it just didn't happen for that team at the time... there seemed to be some sort of a mental block when it came to hurling Cork. I've no idea why that was.'

◄◄◆▷►

AT THE COUNTY convention in 1983, I withdrew my nomination for '84 as I knew Mount Sion would be putting someone forward for involvement with the senior set-up the following year and that it wouldn't be me.

I was very disappointed as I would have like to have stayed involved… and that Mount Sion didn't recognise that they already had someone involved with the senior panel who wanted to stay on, but that was out of my hands. Unfortunately, things got worse for Waterford before they got better at senior level, dropping down to Division Three hurling for the first time following the 1985 campaign.

That had to be our lowest ebb. But my time with Waterford was behind me by then and I'd no real design on being the manager, I must admit. I was better suited to training and coaching.

The manager's job, such as it was at that time, was a glorified position, I felt. It's a lot more defined nowadays and I think it's probably a better structure now. Managing by committee had to go. You need someone, you need an individual who is willing to make a big call on the line and that's often a call that has to be made in the space of a few seconds.

Of course, you'd have a quick consultation with the lads either side of you, you have to respect the men alongside you, but you probably need the one man in charge on the line who will make the big calls.

And that has to be the fella with 'Bainisteoir' printed on his bib.

◄◄◆►►

Jim Greene

'ÓG WAS A very intelligent man when it came to hurling and, on a personal basis, given how strong our friendship was, me being a player and him being a selector didn't interfere in any way, shape or form in terms of how we got on with each other.

'If Óg pointed at an object and told me it was black rather than white, I'd believe him because of the man he was and the experience he had. I was the same with Frankie Walsh. These were men who put their money where their mouth was – they're the ones with the Celtic Crosses – so the notion that I'd challenge either of them on anything never came to mind.

'Óg played hurling when the game was a lot harder, during a time when the game had between 70 and 80 skills… I reckon it's down to 30 now. He had incredible knowledge of the game and he made a huge contribution as both a player and a trainer. The winner's medals speak for themselves.

'Óg was an outstanding hurler and a brilliant tactician. He's an exceptional man by every measure I can think of.

'I love Martin Óg like I loved my own father.'

◄◄◆►►

AFTER THE RUN of success as trainer with Mount Sion, I found myself out on the grass for a while – and Mount Sion didn't lift the *News & Star* Cup again until 1981. There wasn't any particular reason why I wasn't involved again with the seniors or the 21s… trainers were usually appointed at the annual general meeting and someone other than myself during any of those years could have been proposed, as was the candidate's right and the right of the proposer.

That's just how things were and I'd no ill feeling about it or anything. I knew I'd served the club well as both a player and a trainer, and I'd won with pretty much every team I was involved in. But I felt I had more to offer and I saw little point in moping about it, so I became one of the first fellas to go outside of the club to train another team. I was never going to train another team in Waterford, that was never on the cards given the loyalty I'd had to Mount Sion since I was a young fella… so I crossed the Suir for south Kilkenny and began coaching Glenmore, a club with a huge football tradition.

There weren't too many Waterford men after crossing the river to train any Kilkenny club at the time I did it, not that I gave it too much thought at the time. So what I'd learned from Paddy Greene and passed onto the Mount Sion players came with me to Glenmore, who were playing junior hurling at the time.

And what a run I'd have with those players… winning junior, intermediate and senior championships in Kilkenny, tearing up the established order in the county. That was also very satisfying, doing something that had never been done.

I had good lads with me and great lads out on the field. We did something very special together and I'm very proud of that too.

But before I made a decision on training them, I felt I needed to meet them so I went down to Glenmore one night and met the players in the old schoolhouse and there was a fair crowd of them there. Martin Cassin was the chairman of the club at the time and he gave a speech to introduce me, and then indicated that I'd say a few words. But I said, 'No, I won't. I'll ask questions, expect answers and ye (the players) can ask questions of me and I'll try and answer them!'

So I threw the floor open to questions and a chap by the name of Whelan put up his hand and said, 'How do we win the junior championship?'

'That's an easy one to answer,' I told him. 'You do what I tell you.'

Some other voice was raised, with a certain level of scepticism and said, 'What do you mean exactly, about us doing what you tell us?'

So off I went…

'I'm going to be a right Irishman and I'll answer that by asking a question of my own. How many of ye play soccer? Put up your hands if ye're playing soccer.'

I'd say 14 or 15 hands went up.

'Now, ye're all after playing your last soccer match.'

Another player Johnny Murphy put up his hand and told me, 'Martin Óg, I've a cup final this coming Sunday. Can I play that?'

'Ye can do what ye like between now and next Tuesday, but after that, soccer is out!' I answered.

Not one of the lads who met me in the schoolhouse that night played soccer beyond the following Tuesday. They concentrated on hurling and that was a huge part of building that team… they still had junior football, but hurling was the priority.

And my job was to do what I could to make them better.

Christy Heffernan, whose name is as synonymous with Glenmore as anyone who ever hurled for the club, was someone I knew from his time working in the summers as a young fella in Clover Meats where we worked in the same section – and this will surprise no-one – we spent our fair share of time talking about hurling.

◄◄◆►►

Christy Heffernan

'WE WENT FROM junior to senior in a three-year span… and in a 10-year-span, which went beyond Martin Óg's time with us, we were All-Ireland senior club champions, all with the same players.

'It was some rise through the ranks.

'Now, I was one of the older lads within that bunch, but a lot of the lads came up through underage together and it was some run to be a part of.

'Great days. And Martin had an awful lot to do with that success.

'The late Mick Lynch, who was from Valentia Island in Kerry, was a primary schoolteacher in Glenmore. He's an uncle-in-law to Derek McGrath and an uncle of Ger Lynch, who won three All-Ireland football titles with Kerry in the 80s, playing right wing-back.

'Mick had a huge influence on the supply chain of hurlers into the adult team because in the primary school, Mick, a man steeped in football, got all the lads playing hurling. Those lads were together since under-10 grade, whereas in my day we didn't even have an under-14 team... when we went to under-16 we played with Tullogher because we couldn't field a standalone team.

'So Martin got the crop that was coming through in the early 80s, who were after playing in four under-21 'A' county finals, which was unheard of for a Glenmore team previously. So Mick's supply chain and Martin Óg's way of thinking gelled everything together. As well as winning the senior championship with us in 1987 during his second spell with the club, he'd won one with Ballyhale Shamrocks in '85 too when they beat us in the final.

It was a close call for us in 1987... we were well ahead at half-time, but then Ballyhale came back at us like a typical Kilkenny team, mowing us down and cutting into our lead. But we came good in the last five to 10 minutes to win by 4-10 to 3-9... and I played that match with a broken thumb that I got up in Ennis playing Railway Cup.

'The training with Óg was something else.

'At the end of each session, he had one last drill for us... to carry a fella from one side of the pitch to the other on your back. It could be a smaller fella carrying me – and sure a lot of the lads were smaller than me – but we did what we were told and it didn't half build up our calf muscles.

'Martin had a commanding voice in the dressing-room, very deep and very strong and lads listened to him. He used to smoke Players untipped and he'd click his fingers to knock the ashes off the cigarette. I'd worked in the same part of Clover Meats as Martin when I got summer work there, so we were great friends long before he came down to train us.

'You'd inter-county hurlers from Waterford, Kilkenny, Tipperary and Wexford working there – John Sutton from Glenmore, the Buggys from Wexford, Óg of course – and sure they turned our great Factory League teams.

'I knew Óg's ways before he came down to train us and that was definitely a help to me alright. He'd a really good sense of humour and he took things in good spirits. There were a few lads from Piltown working in Clover who knew how to get a good rise out of him by mentioning Mick Kenny, who Martin Óg didn't have a good day on when he marked him in the 1957 All-Ireland final.

'He enjoyed the ribbing, but everyone used to sit back and listen to Óg, who was a great man to relay back stories about matches, incidents and different players. It was always great fun to listen to him... he's always been the best of company, someone you wanted to be around.

'Now he was supervisor in Clover and he had his job to do, but he was always a nice man and he got our respect without ever having to look for it. He has a great knowledge of hurling... sure he did it all on the field himself, and he had a very clear idea of what he wanted from anyone he trained.

'Martin Óg was a legend, even by the time I first met him and he was driving on fellas even at work. He was always a deep thinker, someone who thought out things very well. In the dressing-room, he'd tell you that hurling was a man's game, he'd tell you how he dealt with certain players during his own time and how that, more often than not, he won his own battle and drove on from there.'

◄◄◆►►

AFTER FOUR VERY enjoyable seasons with Glenmore (1980-83), I didn't train anyone the following year. Then one particular evening, I went up to Mullinavat when Ballyhale were playing Rathnure in a tournament match. And as I was walking out of the field after the full-time whistle, I was approached by Brendan Fennelly – part of the most famous hurling family in Ballyhale at the time – to see if I'd train the Shamrocks.

It didn't take too long for me to say yes.

It was a different challenge with Ballyhale than it had been with Glenmore, given the different levels the clubs were operating at when I first trained them. The Shamrocks had won two All-Ireland titles and six Kilkenny Senior Championships since 1978... they were an established outfit and respected all over the country, so that was a case of keeping those players ticking over, which I think I did. But in terms of training them, there was nothing I did with the Shamrocks that I hadn't done with Glenmore.

I worked every player I had hard.

I don't think I flogged anyone but none of them had a handy session with me either. You trained the way you played, that was my approach and I think it served me as a trainer and the lads I trained pretty well over the years. The Ballyhale lads were very solid, a good, honest bunch and they grew up expecting to win.

And they still do.

One night after training, Liam Fennelly came over to me and said, 'I'll tell you one thing, Óg, I'm training harder with Ballyhale than I am with Kilkenny!'

Now, bear in mind that Liam had been captain of Kilkenny when they won the All-Ireland in 1983 and he'd go on to skipper them to their next MacCarthy Cup in 1992.

'Are you joking!' I questioned.

'I'm not,' he replied just as quickly.

That came as a big surprise to me and I've often thought since that Kilkenny's really hard training didn't come in until Brian Cody took over in 1998, and things didn't exactly work out too badly for them after that. I think there's huge merit in players training the way you want them to play.

A bit like Cody, I was never too heavy with the whistle during training matches. If I didn't blow the whistle, it wasn't a free... even though it could well have been. Sometimes you like to test players a bit, to see how they respond to a bit of injustice. If that whistle doesn't blow, unless you're injured, you've just go to get on with things and go with the flow of the game.

I've never seen an umpire raise a flag on account of a player complaining.

I gave two good years with the Shamrocks during which the club won the senior championship in 1985, beating Glenmore in that final (by 4-18 to 3-13) and then the following year, they were beaten in the senior final on what I'd describe as a point of law against Clara. After we'd made a great start, scoring three goals in the first seven minutes, Clara to their credit came back into it and it turned into a real end-to-end match.

We were a point clear with less than five minutes left after Brendan Fennelly struck over a great point from the left of the 'country goal' in Nowlan Park. The game went into injury-time and we still had our noses ahead when Clara's Harry Ryan sent the ball in around the house – to me it looked he was going for a point.

But the ball dropped short and one of their substitutes Joe Casey got a touch on the ball, sent it past Kevin Fennelly and into the net. The referee Dinny Butler went into his umpires to consult – our lads were convinced it was a square ball – but he awarded the goal and soon afterwards blew the final whistle.

Clara, in their first senior final, went home with the cup.

We were hopping. I thought the ref should have blown the final whistle before Harry Ryan sent that ball in towards Kevin. That was a tough one to take and things got a bit heated after the teams made their way off the field.

◄◄◆►►

Kevin Fennelly

'MARTIN ÓG WAS one of several trainers we had during that great period of success for the Shamrocks, when we reached 12 out of 13 Kilkenny senior finals. During that spell, we'd had several top-class trainers, such as Tom Ryan, and we were used to having trainers who'd run all night alongside the players during sessions, but that wasn't Martin Óg's style.

'He stood on the field, gave his instructions and we followed them.

'His philosophy was straightforward… you had to match your opponent's physically and then you had to out-hurl them. And he had a very uncomplicated message, "Do it my f***ing way and you'll win!"'

'And sure enough, as we did for most of the men who trained us at that time, we won the Senior Championship the first year Óg was involved and lost out at the death the following year to Clara. And then Óg went back to Glenmore and they beat us in the final the year after that.

'I'd a really good relationship with Óg.

'He's a bit of a character and he had his own way of doing things as a trainer. He was a great man to get a panel fit and he recognised how important good physical conditioning was. There were a few drills Óg did that were unique to him… some I was keen on, others not so much.

'You'd do your five laps at the start of a session and that always gave him a good gauge as to how we were faring… you never even thought about cutting a corner when Martin Óg sent you off to do your laps.

'Then he'd have us sprint out to the 13-metre line, roll over… then sprint back to the endline, and then have us sprint to the 21-metre line… roll again and back to the end line. That one seemed to suit me, maybe on account of me being in goal and going to ground a bit more than most of the lads would over the course of a match.

'Anyway, that one I'd no issue with. But he'd have us clearing the railing on the side of the field and then scurrying back under the next railing, and I was always relieved at the end of that drill. I never remotely enjoyed that part of training but I never ducked it. We always put the work in.

'As players, we'd always find a way to inject a bit of craic into the toughest of sessions and it was no different when it came to Óg. One night, we were quietly wondering how often he'd swear from one end of the session to the other… Óg used to 'eff' fairly liberally.

'That night, he swore 58 times and we had a quiet laugh about it as he was putting us through our paces. I was glad of any distraction when I was clearing the railing on the side of the field!

'Óg had strong opinions on hurling – he still does – and he was never afraid to express a view about what he expected from us when he trained us, or when we crossed that white line on a Sunday. He had high standards, we did too so it was a good match for the two years he was with us. Martin Óg has never been short on confidence… I'm hardly the first person who's ever said that, but I've always had enormous respect and a huge amount of time for him.

'Hurling people all over the country respect and admire Óg.'

◂◂◆▸▸

TO MOVE ON from Mount Sion and train Glenmore and Ballyhale to senior championships in Kilkenny was very satisfying. But the success with Glenmore was very special, to take a junior team through the ranks to senior status and then to win the senior championship in 1987 was fantastic.

The *Kilkenny People* preview suggested the Shamrocks, fuelled by the outcome of the previous year's final and the winning tradition they'd established over the previous 10 years, would have too much for Glenmore in the '87 Kilkenny final. But Glenmore produced their best performance of that year for when it mattered most, winning by 4-10 to 3-9.

We were 3-9 to 1-4 clear after 38 minutes and we looked well on our way but, of no great surprise to me, the Shamrocks were far from done for and the sides were level by the 51st minute. John Knox, reporting for the *Kilkenny People*, filed the following about the closing stages of the match:

Then Glenmore pulled off a masterstroke and brought Christy Heffernan to centre-forward. He kept his head when all around him were losing theirs, and with a few deft touches, he turned the tide. History was made...

'This day, November 1, 1987 belonged to gutsy Glenmore. Inexperience of the big time, and the big time pressure, nearly cost them the title. They can thank their returned son from Blackrock (Cork), Christy Heffernan. In the end the things he did were simple. But then hurling is a simple game. What he did was he used his experience. It made the difference.

To be involved with any team which does something for the first time is something any player or trainer would be naturally proud of.... and those Glenmore lads couldn't have given me anymore. They well and truly emptied the tank and got their just rewards.

After the match, I told John Knox:

'For a while, I thought we were going to lose. We appeared to get the jitters when the Shamrocks started to come back. We were doing all the small things wrong. In the last few minutes it all came right again. Games like this don't do anything for my heart. I would say 10 years were taken off my life watching that match.'

◄ ◄ ◆ ► ►

Christy Heffernan

'MARTIN ÓG WAS one of the first to come over from Waterford to train a team in Kilkenny and several more followed to Glenmore, including Jim Greene and Tom Casey, so the rapport between our club and Waterford has always been good.

'Glenmore had trainers from Wexford as well, such as Martin Byrne and Dave Guiney, so we've benefited from looking outwards. To go from winning the county junior title in 1980 to All-Ireland senior champions in '91... and to win four senior championships between '87 and '95 was a great achievement. To be captain of the 1987 team after coming back from my year with Blackrock in Cork, with three of my brothers on the team, was a huge honour for me.

'Nothing compares to winning with your club... even winning the All-Ireland with Kilkenny. To win with the lads you grew up with is so special. And we had a man training us who had an aura about him, someone who didn't believe in a hiding place out on a hurling field. I've nothing only good things to say about Martin Óg Morrissey.

'Top class on and off the pitch.'

◀ ◁ ◆ ▷ ▶

AFTER SIX GREAT years training in south Kilkenny, by which time I was in my early fifties, I came back across the river and gave the Butlerstown and Tramore clubs a hand. To this day, it surprises me that hurling doesn't have a heavy footprint in Tramore in terms of a team competing consistently at intermediate level, one that wouldn't be far off the senior grade most years.

When you take the population of Tramore into account, you'd wonder what's missing there but in no way am I pointing the finger at the club alone there. For one thing, you'd have a lot of parents bringing their children back into the city to play for the club the parents played for in their own childhoods.

Boys and girls living in Tramore should be playing hurling, camogie and football for the Tramore club. But as long as there's no parish rule in Waterford, you'd wonder what will make things change on that front. You'd wonder if we were getting more out of Tramore might that be the thing that could get us over the line when it comes to winning another senior All-Ireland Championship.

I knew when my time was up as a trainer.

I didn't need anyone calling to the house for an awkward conversation or anything like that. I realised it was enough for me to be going to matches as a supporter instead of being involved as a trainer and everything that went with that. So off I went with Paddy Murphy... his son Jim who used to drive us and Stephen Greene and no matter where a match was on, bar ones in the Six Counties, off we went watching Waterford... and a good time was had by all.

By then, I felt I'd put enough into hurling to sit back, relax and enjoy the game in a way that you can't really do when you're either playing or training a team.

My only regret?

That I didn't have a lengthier involvement with the Waterford senior team and that my single year with them wasn't more successful than it was. But all in all, between Mount Sion, Glenmore and Ballyhale Shamrocks, when you weight everything up… I didn't do too badly.

There was plenty of good hurling played, a level of success along the way and many a good friendship made on both sides of the Suir.

Great days… and I'm grateful for all of them.

After his playing days, Martin Óg proved himself just as successful on the sideline and although his career in the Waterford hotseat was short, he made an impact on so many players in his own county and in clubs in Kilkenny, including Jim Greene and Kevin Fennelly (above), and the Glenmore and Kilkenny great Christy Heffernan (below).

« CHAPTER 11 »

In Homage to the Hurley

Sometimes you can go through months without breaking a hurl, and then you can break two or three in one match. It's hard to know, you can't really plan for it – but you always try and have three, four, five that you like with you at all times. There's nothing worse than breaking your favourite hurl, nothing worse – it's heartbreak.

– Neil McManus (*The Irish Times*, August 6, 2019)

MY FIRST FEW hurleys were sourced from a fella called Cahill out in Mount Congreve Estate and Gardens, a few miles outside of Waterford city. He lived in the gate lodge next to the main entrance.

He used to gather the ash from around the estate to make his hurleys… all by hand, and I bought mine for half a crown, which was about one-eighth of an old Irish pound at that stage. Some of the hurleys he made you could nearly use as a belt on your trousers… they were fantastic.

I got my hurleys from him up until I started playing in the Juvenile League. I then started getting my hurleys over the bridge from Petey Walsh in Dunkitt. He made one particular hurley for my brother Mattie and it was a lovely stick, but Mattie didn't want it as he felt it was too short for him… so I took it.

I was 12 years old and it was the best hurley I'd ever played with up to that point. It's funny the way some things stick in your head. Well that hurley certainly has.

BY THE TIME I was playing for Mount Sion, both the club and Waterford were sourcing their hurleys from Randall's in Wexford, while there was also a chap by the name of Ireland on the way into Kilkenny that I used to get hurleys from for a while. And the last place I got hurleys from while I was playing was Falconer's in Piltown, who are still going.

Now, there was another man in town who used to make hurleys when I was a young fella – Raymie Dowling – but I rarely mastered his hurleys until one day when I was still in school, when we were going up training one Tuesday to the Sportsfield (Walsh Park), two days after a Waterford/Kilkenny match.

I used to get the key for the field off Bobby Kennedy, the groundsman… it was one of those keys that could open any lock. Well, in I went and I opened the door of the shed and what was facing me only a brand new hurley. So I picked that up… and it was mine!

But that was the only hurley Raymie made that I mastered. It's hard to explain now what made it feel so different then… all I knew is that it felt different as soon as I got hold of it.

One of the nicest hurleys I ever got was from Tom Penkert in Ferrybank, who was a distant relative of mine, just before we hurled Limerick down in Cork. He was one of the county board's Munster Council delegates. He said he'd a lovely hurley for me but he couldn't give it to me until before the match in Cork because the Waterford minor goalkeeper Percy Flynn was using it in the match before we played.

Well, the stroke I got out of that hurley once I got my hands on it was something else… 80 yards off the ground. It was a gorgeous stick.

We were training above in the field one evening and there used to be a fair old crowd watching us, including a lot of old lads who'd have played for Waterford years beforehand. One of them came out to me as training ended and asked could he borrow my hurley for a few pucks. Ten minutes later, he walked into me with the hurley in two pieces.

I could have killed him, but he was very apologetic about it and I got over it soon enough. But if I'd to pick a favourite hurley, I'd have to go with a Randall. That was the brand I used longer than any other over all the years I played.

WATTIE MORRISSEY FROM Griffith Place was one of the taxi drivers with the county team and he used to go down to Randall's to get the hurleys for us. I could be walking along the street – Wattie drove an oil lorry at the time – and I'd get a shout, 'Hey, Óg, call up at half two, I've two hurleys for you!'

Wattie knew exactly what I wanted.

He might have brought two dozen hurleys back from Wexford with him but he always put two to one side for me. The weight and the grain of the stick were my two top considerations when it came to finding the right hurley.

I remember being up in the field one night at training when Philly Grimes asked for a look at my hurley, so I handed it to him.

'Ah, Jesus!' said Philly. 'If I was using that, I'd want an ass to carry it round with me!' Compared to the rest of the lads, I used a heavier hurley. A light hurley was no good to me as I'd be first-time pulling, so I needed something substantial. Usually, we all had two hurleys, with Wattie holding one in reserve for each of us during a match, and he was always on hand to replace the broken hurley.

I don't ever remember any of us ever getting someone else's spare… Wattie ran a tight ship and he always had a few lads helping him along the different lines of the field between backs, midfielders and forwards, and they switched ends just like we did during a match. The system worked well for us.

I always kept my hurleys at home, in the coal shed underneath the stairs. I got two bands put on the bas and after the bands went on, I always oiled the hurley with raw linseed oil and I left it soak into it.

It might be six months before I'd use a hurley the way I treated them… it'd get more than one coat after the initial job too, and you'd have it done in a few minutes. Only a few of us used to do that at the time. For want of a better phrase, it kept the hurley 'damp' whereas most other fellas' hurleys would be dry.

And I can tell you, when it came to the clash of the ash, the damp one always came out on top.

Traditionally, the 'heel' of the hurley used to be sharp. Around the time I started playing minor hurling, I used to run the right side of that heel along a concrete wall and put a bit of a curve on it. So when I was taking a cut or hitting the ball off the ground, the hurley wouldn't 'catch' the surface on me after I'd struck the ball.

I didn't know anyone else who did that while I was playing. It really made a difference for me… I felt I made a better, cleaner connection with the sliotar once I started treating the hurley that way.

In the drawn 1959 All-Ireland final, the goal that Seamus Power scored to bring us level with Kilkenny was from a sideline cut that I took… and I was on the 'far-off' side of the pitch from Seamus, the Cusack Stand side, when I cut it and it went all the way into him. There's been a lot of talk in the past five or 10 years whenever a modern inter-county player cuts a ball over the bar, but I remember scoring one myself from 50 yards out against Limerick.

We didn't practice cuts the way we should have back then and certainly not the way Joe Canning clearly did since he was a young fella, but between strength, a good eye and a quality hurley, we had our moments back in my day.

And all of mine were made possible by a treated, 'damp' hurley.

Martin Óg relished his time in the blue of Munster, playing alongside some of the game's all-time greats.

« CHAPTER 12 »

Martin Óg on...

THE BEST PLAYER HE EVER MARKED
CORK'S PADDY BARRY.

I always found him a handful and I don't know why, even now.

A few lads in Cork told me that Paddy reckoned he was better than Christy Ring, but I suppose you'd have to have the confidence of a Corkman to declare you were better than Ring! Paddy was a big, strong man and well able to hurl.

Look, you're always going to meet someone better than you out on the field and Paddy was most definitely my bogeyman. I never instigated any chat with Paddy or anyone I played for that matter, be it with Mount Sion or Waterford.

I always maintained that whenever a forward started talking to me that he was trying to put me off my game, trying to lull me into a false sense of security. To be fair, not many ever did that to me… and Paddy certainly didn't. B

ut by God, he kept me occupied.

WHAT MADE CHRISTY RING SPECIAL
YOU'D NEVER GET the end of Ring.

I think there was a match between Dublin and Cork when Ring was marked by a fella called Des 'Snitchy' Ferguson, and for 50 minutes, Snitchy was outstanding and then he passed some remark to Ring.

In a handful of minutes, Ring had two or three balls in the back of the net.

You had to sit on Ring the whole time… if your concentration lapsed at all, he'd be waiting for that moment and more often than not he capitalised on it. Whenever the ball came into his vicinity, you knew Ring was always going to look for it.

He wasn't like TJ Reid, Henry Shefflin, Jimmy Doyle or DJ Carey for that matter… someone who would ghost away with the ball out of a melee and then strike the ball over the bar. Ring would be in the middle of the melee, looking for the ball.

And he had some pair of wrists on him too… he could brilliantly flick the ball into another forward's path.

Ring was something else.

MICK KENNY IN THE 1957 ALL-IRELAND FINAL

THAT WAS THE toughest day I had on any Kilkenny man during my inter-county career. I coughed up a few soft scores to him but they counted every bit as much as the harder earned scores Kilkenny engineered that day.

The Irish Press match report the following morning noted:

Martin Óg Morrissey did his utmost to curb the crafty Kenny.

To me, I still feel like Kenny didn't have a particularly great game, yet he ended up scoring 2-5 in the final so that put him on a pedestal and he finished the year as the championship's top scorer with 3-18. He clearly did something right.

But it's fair to say the 1957 final isn't a day I've too many fond memories of. Losing that day still annoys me more than losing in '63.

WHAT IT TAKES TO WIN

WELL, YOU'LL WIN nothing for being nice.

It takes steel to win matches. All the great teams in any sport take to the field with at least one barrel loaded. The week before the 1963 National League final against Tipperary, a phone call came into me from the gate at Clover Meats, from John D Hickey of the Irish Independent.

So down I went, picked up the phone and spoke to John and he asked me, 'What about Sunday?'

'I think we'll win by about three or four points,' I replied.

John said back to me, 'Well, Mackey McKenna (of Tipperary) said you gave him a good roasting in the Oireachtas final but that he's going to give you a roasting next Sunday'.

'Well of course he's entitled to his opinion,' I told him. 'But I still think we'll win by three or four points.'

The first ball in that league final that came into us, both of us pulled on it and by the time he looked at his hurley, Mackey had about two inches of the stick left in his hand. I gave him another roasting that day – if I say so myself – and we won by two points.

GOING IN HARD

I USED WHATEVER weight I had – I was 12 stone at my playing peak – as best I could when I tackled. But I had what I'd call a happy knack of hitting a fella when he was on the 'off-leg'… by that I mean, the leg he had less weight on when challenging for the ball.

And the very minute you'd tip him on the off-leg, nine times out of 10 he'd end up on the ground. I remember trying to explain this to two lads out on the training pitch alongside Fraher Field one evening. I caught one of the lads by the right hand and asked him to plant his right leg on the ground and leave his left leg off the ground… and then I got the other lad to tackle him on the off-leg side.

Well down he went, just as I thought he would. He took it in great spirits and we all had a good laugh about it. But that's how you tackle effectively.

There's no point going in bald-headed.

If you're thinking about what you're going to do with the ball once you have it – are you going to go long with a pass, short with a pass or shoot for a score – you should spend as much time thinking about how you'll tackle an opponent. You have to identify the weakest point and then do your best to exploit that weakness.

And the off-leg tackle only needs to be a tip to be effective. You don't need to be going in like a wrecking ball.

I tried to do just that most of the time I played.

A FEW ALTERCATIONS

IF YOU GO out onto the field angry, I don't think it's going to end too well for you. Staying calm is very important and, fair enough, you know you need to be aggressive, but it has to be controlled aggression.

In my time playing, I lost my head twice – once as a junior player and once as a senior. Now I saw the line as a minor as well but nothing, in my mind, happened to justify me being sent off. And Tom Cheasty was put off alongside me... he was playing for Dunhill O'Brien's at that grade.

There wasn't a dirty stroke pulled by either of us. It looked like Tom was coming at me with his hurley but I caught it, pulled it out of his hand and threw it away. But the referee sent the two of us off. After the two of us went in and got dressed, Tom came back out and stood on the line with his crowd and somebody, I suspect, must have been egging him on because he ended up back out on the field and clattered one of our players, a fella called Davern.

Shortly afterwards, I think Tom was suspended for life. It actually could have been worse only for an intervening leg by Ger McCarthy which prevented Tom from making an even heavier contact than he did on Davern.

That saved Tom from a world of trouble.

The day I was sent off in a junior match out in Portlaw, two of us pulled on a ball – the other fella being a Kiely from Portlaw. It was a greasy day and the two of us hit the ball dead on. I went out to go after the ball when I got a wallop of a hurley and if I did, well I just turned around and let fly.

So off I went.

Twelve months later, didn't I meet 'Kielo' and he said to me, 'Hey, Martin Óg, you nearly destroyed me that day out in Portlaw when you hit me.'

'Sure weren't you looking for it?' I told him.

He said back to me, 'Well, I suppose I was... I passed blood after it. Anyway, I'm sorry... I thought it was your brother that was in it.'

The third sending off was against Erin's Own in the 1962 senior final, which probably stopped us winning 10 successive senior championships. I thought the two of us should have gone that day but the ref only saw my retaliation.

Three blips over 20-odd years wasn't too bad, given where I hurled. And I never saw the line with Waterford.

KNOWING HIS ROLE

I COULD READ the game very well from left-half-back... for me it's the ideal position on a hurling field. The very minute the opposition goalkeeper or one of their inside set of backs hit a ball, I could tell by the shape of the fella striking the ball where it'd land within two or three feet of where it ended up.

So I was moving to meet that ball and be in that area as soon as the ball was struck, and that's not something I see too many in the same position doing in the modern game. When I hear analysts on television referring to the sweeper, it makes me laugh.

In hurling and football, and it has always been the case, there are three sweepers in every team… and they're all in the half-back line. The centre-back, at some stage during any game, is going to end up covering for his two wing-backs and vice versa.

I'd a chat not so long with a retired centre-back from Carrick-on-Suir about the difference in the style of play now compared to what it was when I was playing… and my half of the conversation was all about how I think a half-back line should play.

Back in the days when the great Mick Roche, God rest him, played centrefield for the Carrick Davins – he was centre-back for Tipperary in his prime – but the chap playing centre-back for the Davins would tap the ball out under the opposition puck out and Mick always knew what he was going to do with it… tap it out to Roche.

'I was finished with the ball then and it was Mick's problem after that,' he told me with a big laugh.

THE TUSSLES WITH TIPPERARY

THE TROUNCING IN 1958 was probably the lowpoint of the '57–'63 period with Waterford but we put that right the following year when we beat them out the gate in the Munster semi-final by 9-3 to 3-4, having led 8-2 without reply at half-time.

What a day that was. God, we didn't half stick it to them.

Before the match, we went to The Metropole Hotel for a cup of team and a sandwich. I told a few of the boys that I had to use the facilities, so off I went to the gents. The toilets in the hotel took up a fair bit of floorspace and there were two doors going into it… and I went in one door and then out the other. Larry Guinan and Frankie Walsh went in there, looking for me and they thought I was still using one of the cubicles which had a door on it.

They got a half bucket of water and threw it in over the door… and who was in there, only Tony Wall from Tipperary! The two lads took off like bullets and it was only afterwards we found who exactly was in there.

But there was no formal enquiry after that!

That Tipp team – outside of Tipp anyway – had a pretty bad name at the time. I saw them do things that they shouldn't have done, but if you did the same back to them, then they left you alone. Hitting them first was important.

On that Tipp team, from 1962 to '66 you had the full-back line of John Doyle, Michael Maher and Kieran Carey, who later came to be known as 'Hell's Kitchen' by John D Hickey. Doyle, with his tongue in his cheek said, and I heard him saying it myself when the three of them retired from hurling, that they could close the hospital in Nenagh!

They were tough, no two ways about it.

They stood on ceremony for no one. If a clout could stop you scoring a goal, then you got a clout. John Doyle once said, 'I'll put it this way, we got as much punishment as we were supposed to have handed out. I can assure you of that'.

I have to say I loved beating Tipp.

It felt like a bigger feather in my cap than beating Kilkenny, probably on account of my parents being from Kilkenny. Tipp were the kingpins around that time and we beat them four times in the one year… and it wasn't just sweet.

It was gorgeous.

HIS WATERFORD TEAM'S QUALITIES

IN TERMS OF hurling, I think the Waterford team that I played with had a style of their own. We played fast, open hurling. I remember being at a wedding a couple of years ago down in Cork and a chap walked over to me, shook my hand and said, 'I watched ye playing hurling, and the hurling ye played was the best I ever saw'.

I don't think the fellas of the present day would stand up to the type of hurling we played. Handpassing is now a plague on the game. I'd do away with it completely if I had anything to do with hurling. The game is called hurling, not handball and so many of the handpasses are thrown balls too… I can't stick it.

I'll be honest, I'd rather watch a camogie match some days because there's more actual hurling played in a lot of those games than in what the men now serve up.

MIXING WITH INTER-COUNTY TEAMMATES

WE SOCIALISED IN our way… I can't imagine we were much different from how other panels mixed at the time. In 1962/63 we beat Wexford in a National League play-off in Kilkenny and after the match we headed for the Metropole Hotel above there.

There were six or seven Mount Sion players on the panel and Johnny Kiely from Dungarvan was sat at the same table as us, and we were sitting down chatting about the match… and sure we were naturally in good form after winning the match and we were all chatting away. Then a fella walked over to where we were sitting and said there were some celebrations going on over in Bonner's, which was a public house at the time and it was only around the corner.

So we decided, Johnny and all, to go and have a look at what was going on. And who was in there only the Wexford team…every single one of them, and they were all having a drink, a sing-song and everything.

I turned around to our fellas with a big smile and said, 'Did we win the match or did they win it?' It'll tell you the difference between the club teams and the county team in Waterford at the time.

When we were coming out of Bonner's, Johnny Kiely tapped me on the shoulder and said, 'I didn't think ye were such a nice crowd of fellas!' I'd great time for Johnny. No matter where I passed him after that or if he passed me in his van when he was out on a job up in Waterford, Johnny would pull in and we have an auld chat for a half an hour or so. He was a nice man.

THE SLUMP IN WATERFORD'S FORTUNES POST-1963

THERE WAS ONE last Munster final appearance for the surviving members of the 1957-63 era in 1966 when we lost to Cork by 4-9 to 2-9 in Limerick. That Cork side went on to win the All-Ireland title after beating Kilkenny by 3-9 to 1-10. As for why we slid out of contention and ended up winning nothing for 39 years, well I wouldn't be laying any blame at any county board official's door for that.

I think you'd have to look at the players before you'd look at anything or anyone else. Did as many of the lads that followed us put it in as hard as all of us did when we were at our peak? Or was it just a case that while many a good player wore the Waterford jersey after our time passed that there just wasn't as many good players in the county?

Maybe a few of us from our team should have had a bit more input with the senior panels that followed after we retired. I still think I could tell a young lad nowadays a thing or two about the game and how to handle himself. Whether any of them would listen or not is another thing entirely, of course.

I know I had my year with the panel in 1983, but I'd have liked a bit more time with them. I think I'd a bit more to offer the county and I think my time with Glenmore and Ballyhale underlined that. I'd have liked to manage Waterford but that's all water under the bridge now.

THE BEST WATERFORD PLAYERS HE'S SEEN
SINCE HIS RETIREMENT

TO BE FAIR, there's been a few good ones since 1970.

You've Pat McGrath, Tony Browne and Ken McGrath from my own club... and Paul Flynn from Ballygunner. They're some who come immediately to mind.

I can't help thinking that all the while we've had too many nice hurlers and that if they'd had a bit more devilment in them, that we'd have at least two All-Irelands won since 1998.

BALLYGUNNER, JUSTIN MCCARTHY AND
WATERFORD POST-1998

IN THE LAST few years, Ballygunner have walked through the county championship, but in 2021 they did actually get a fright off Mount Sion – I think Mount Sion left it behind them as a matter of fact – but that one game aside, Ballygunner have strolled through match after match. But that hasn't automatically transferred into success, then, for the inter-county team and why that has been the case, I don't know.

To have a good county team, you'll have to have at least one strong club team in the county. And whether the current Waterford team is good enough to win an All-Ireland, again, I don't know... I have my doubts and why that is... Tony Browne, Ken McGrath, Paul Flynn and so on, you're talking about great hurlers who gave great service to Waterford down through the years. But taking the whole team into account, to me, I don't think they responded well enough to the rougher stuff.

That 1998 semi-final against Kilkenny was definitely one that got away. It was a low scoring game and I don't think we made the best decisions on the sideline that day. Offaly in the final wouldn't have been the same prospect as Clare by then… I don't think there's too much argument about that. During Justin McCarthy's time here, we definitely had enough talent to win an All-Ireland. He was a great man to get the team ready, a very good trainer, but I don't think his decision making was always the best once the team was out on the pitch and the game was on.

Again, like the man before him in the job, I think Justin was a bit reluctant to take a fella off or to make a positional switch at critical times during matches.

STRENGTH IN DEPTH

WHEN YOU TAKE most of the teams that are after winning All-Irelands over the past 20 or so years – Kilkenny, Tipperary and Limerick – they've all had fellas on the sideline that are every bit as good as the fellas named to start. But, to be fair, in Waterford, we haven't had that… we've tended to have 11 to 12 really good players in our starting teams since 1998 – but then you have a bit of a 'tail' on the team.

I don't think I've ever seen a Waterford team, even our team in 1959, that had 15 stars on it… there was always some little flaw in some part of the team, even on our best days. It's very hard to have all 15 fellas flying on a big day, but that tends to be what you need if you want to win an All-Ireland title.

WHY SIZE MATTERS

WHEN YOU THINK about the game now and look at the Limerick team, there must be 11 of their starting team over six feet tall and no matter what way you look at it, a good big man is better than a good small man any day of the week. And the only way you'll beat them, I feel, is with the type of hurling we used to play, because the ball would be going helter skelter the whole time.

Down through all the years, there's rarely been a Waterford team which has physically dominated their opponents.

A SOMETIMES TENSE RELATIONSHIP WITH MOUNT SION

I THINK THE hierarchy within the club didn't accept me the way the players did. Quite why that was, I'm not 100 percent sure. I've always had a strong personality and there was no shortage of strong personalities among those running the club so maybe it was just a case of oil and water... sure, even the man above couldn't mix those two.

One year, ahead of the AGM, I was approached about letting my name go forward to chair the club. I was up for it and was happy to let my name go into the hat. The night before the AGM, the bell rang at home and there was a friend of mine who wanted to come in and have a chat about the AGM.

'I'm advising you now to withdraw your name,' he said. 'There's going to be a few big guns going up against you.' I quickly made a decision and the following night when my name was mentioned, I raised my hand and withdrew my candidacy. That was very disappointing.

While I'm no stranger to extolling my own virtues, I still felt I had a lot to offer the club. But I'll remain a proud Mount Sion man until the bell tolls.

EDDIE KEHER
A PURE ARTIST with a hurley. An outstanding player, pure and simple.

THE BEST BACKS HE EVER SAW
(MARTIN ÓG COULDN'T NOMINATE HIMSELF!)
EXCLUDING MYSELF REALLY narrowed my options!

Ah, I saw many a good one, but it's very hard to pick one above the other. The two Rackards (Wexford), Nick O'Donnell (Kilkenny), Jimmy Finn and John Doyle (both Tipperary) and John Lyons (Cork), sure they were all outstanding.

And sure you can't have a conversation like this without mentioning our own man, John Keane.

HIS GALWAY FAN CLUB
AFTER RTE'S Up For The Match TV programme finished in 2017, Larry Guinan and myself went for a drink afterwards. As I stood at the counter, a Galway man approached me and declared, 'Let me shake hands with a legend'.

It was Sylvie Linnane, one of only four Galwaymen to hold three All-Ireland winners' medals – and my goodness he was no slouch out on the field. Talk about a tough bit of stuff.

In my time, Jimmy Hegarty was the Galway goalkeeper and a few years back he visited Waterford and a chap called Mossie Power from Ferrybank brought Jimmy over to say hello. We'd never met socially before but we had a cup of tea and a good old chat about hurling.

'In Galway, you're reckoned to be the first pure "hurling centre-back ever", he said, to which I replied, 'What do you mean?'

'Most of the fellas who'd played in that position before you were only mullockers. But a lot of Galway people reckoned you were something different.'

Needless to say, I didn't contradict the claim Jimmy brought into my living room! But that was some bit of praise to get.

HIS RELATIVELY BRIEF REFEREEING CAREER

I REMEMBER GOING up to Bansha one time and a chap of the Moloneys from Tipperary was refereeing a match up there. I was after doing a couple of matches here in Waterford and Pat Fanning, who travelled with me, introduced me to Moloney before the match and told him that, 'Óg is after refereeing a few matches'. And Moloney asked me what I made of it?

I told him, 'I think ye have the game destroyed'.

'What do you mean?' he said.

'The player in possession is only allowed three steps with the ball in his hand. After that, you should be blowing for a free.'

And that, for me, was where most of the trouble in hurling has persisted right up to the present day. I said to Moloney, 'A fella goes too far with the ball in his hand and if somebody hits him and takes him out of the game, the fella with the ball gets the free. If you'd blown it after he's gone more than three steps with the ball in his hand, the free would be awarded the other way round.'

He went out and he blew the whistle twice in the first 10 minutes for fellas over-carrying the ball and I can only recall two to three more frees being blown during the rest of the match after that.

In the early 70s, when I was still playing, I dabbled in refereeing. I think that's the best way to describe it. I was going into Mass one day and the secretary of the Waterford County Board at the time came over to me and asked would I referee the Sargent Cup final that afternoon between Portlaw and Dunhill, two neighbouring parishes. He couldn't find anyone to ref it, apparently.

So I said I would on condition that he was to go into both dressing-rooms and instruct both teams that if there was any dirty play, I'd not hesitate to show anyone the line. He said he couldn't do that, so I decided I'd do that myself out on the field before the throw-in by calling them all into to the middle of the pitch.

'I'm the boss. I'm the man with the whistle!' I told both teams. 'If you make mistakes that I think are fouls, then I'll blow the whistle. If I make mistakes, there'll be f**k all any of you can do about that… and you'll just have to put up with it.'

In the first half hour, I gave Portlaw's Martin Hickey the advantage twice and he scored two goals. The game was only after restarting in the second-half when Martin was fouled but I gave him the advantage again and he pulled his shot wide.

He turned around and said, 'Ah, ref, ref!'

I called him over and said, 'Come here, I want you… I gave you the advantage twice in the first half hour and you scored two goals from there. Did you want me to blow the whistle, terminate this game and start afresh without any concessions?'

Martin replied, 'Oh, no, no, no.'

'Keep that shut then,' I told him.

I remember sending a fella off in a junior match. He'd pulled across someone and he had to go and I told him, 'You're acting the cowboy, so get off your horse and go to the sideline!' In the long run, I didn't get into refereeing too much and maybe that's just as well.

I reckon I'd have been too strict.

THOUGHTS ON MODERN HURLING

I'M A BIT stumped trying to pick out what I like about the game today, to be honest. I actually don't know if there's something I like more about inter-county hurling now when I compare it to the game we played and the way we used to play it.

I'll answer it like this… the elements that we excelled in, like overhead hurling, ground hurling and first-time hurling, they're all gone now. I don't think the game is a better one without the three of them. Faster and stronger doesn't necessarily mean better.

I'm not enamoured with the way Limerick have played over the last three-to-five years given their reliance on the handpass and how they used it to open up the play. The first team I can recall playing like that was Ballygunner inside the past

10 years… it doesn't seem to matter who is doing the scoring. But both of them have been very successful and they both really play as teams.

Limerick have really brought it to a fine art to win three in-a-row All-Irelands, so you'd have to say that shows how well coached they are.

To a lesser extent, Kilkenny have introduced that game as well, and when Tipperary have been on top of their game over the past 10 years, they've produced a similar style of hurling. You certainly can't find fault with the attitude of Limerick, just as you couldn't with all the different Kilkenny teams Brian Cody picked.

They have found a way that works and that way is winning provincial and All-Ireland titles. And here we are in Waterford, after a few close shaves over the past 20 or so years and we still haven't climbed the mountain. To see 11, 12 fellas around the ball and they trying to pick it up drives me crazy. Then the ball gets thrown back in by the ref… and the same 11, 12 fellas are still standing there and you end up with another ruck.

There should be only two players anywhere near a thrown ball and no-one else bar the ref within 14 or even 21 yards of the restart. If the refs started dishing out cards for anyone who encroaches, players wouldn't take too long to change their habits.

The game remains strong, thankfully, but it has changed a lot.

There's an awful fuss made out of inter-county teams nowadays playing four weeks running and a lot of talk about players being tired and so on. I can remember playing five matches in seven days, seven-a-side on three of those days… and we all enjoyed it. I don't remember anyone saying it was too much or anything like that.

I certainly don't think that playing every weekend is detrimental. When we played, we were told that the more matches you played, the better you got… that the best training you'd ever have was during a match.

THE MODERN SLIOTAR

IF OLLIE WALSH was playing today in goal for Kilkenny, he'd be putting puck outs the length of the field and over the bar. Something needs to be done about the ball. It's not that it's too light necessarily, but what it's made up of now seems to make it carry a lot further than what it did when I was playing.

There was a Brother Hickey in Mount Sion who made sliotars – I had one of them somewhere, whatever I did with it – and you could leave it out on a wet day and the rain would make no difference to it, the ball didn't get heavy.

The Lawlor number one was a smallish ball and that was the best ball that I ever played with and even on wet days it never got that heavy.

THE BEST HURLER OF THE PAST 60 YEARS

FOR ME, IT'S Jimmy Doyle, the 'Boy Wonder' from Thurles, Tipperary's All-Ireland winning captain in both 1962 and '65. Believe it or not, he won his last senior championship with Thurles Sarsfields – his 10th in total – in 1974, the same year I won my last county title with Mount Sion.

There can't have been a game he played for Tipp that he didn't score in. I remember talking to him in the Mount Sion Centre and he pointed out the scars on his forehead and face. 'I didn't get any of them playing with Tipperary,' he told me. 'I got them playing in Tipperary.'

After Jimmy died in 2015, Babs Keating was interviewed on RTE and he mentioned a conversation he'd had many years previously with Christy Ring:

'I used to have lunch with Christy once a fortnight. This particular day in Mallow, a few people came over to talk about hurling. They threw a question at me, "Who is the best hurler ever in your opinion?" I wouldn't answer in Christy's presence but we were walking out afterwards to the car and Christy walked beside me, shrugged his shoulders and said. "Do you know what, Babs, if Jimmy Doyle was as strong as you and I… no one would ever ask who was the greatest hurler". Probably the greatest compliment that was ever paid to any hurler.'

Ring knew. Jimmy was magic.

THE BEST WATERFORD PLAYER HE EVER PLAYED WITH

I THINK IT would have to be Philly Grimes.

Himself and Seamus Power were such a brilliant centrefield combination; we've never had a better pair in that position for Waterford since. Philly was all hurling. I had some view of his class on the field… sure we were never too far apart most matches. If you ever did something well yourself, Philly, without fail, would run over and tap you on the shoulder and then urge you to do it again. And he was a great athlete.

He had it all.

And I'm far from the only person who has ever said that.

Jim Greene

'WHILE ÓG HAS never had any problem talking about himself – and that's something I admire about him, by the way – Grimes loved talking about hurling but he never spoke about himself, how great a player he was and what he did.

'He never gave himself any credit other than acknowledging that he was part of that great Waterford team. I was so close with Óg that he was always my favourite. But Philly was the favourite with thousands of Waterford supporters. He was magical.

'He lit up the field the minute he came onto it and he ran on his toes.

'In the 1962 Oireachtas final, Ned Power pucked out the ball… and this a known fact, Grimes was at centrefield, took off heading towards the Tipperary goal, looked back over his shoulder, caught the ball in full stride and struck it over the bar.

'A phenomenal talent."

Bridie Barron

'OH MY GOD, Philly was some hurler.

'Sure we were reared with the Grimeses; a lot of people couldn't tell who was a Grimes and who was a Morrissey. When poor Philly was dying, God be merciful to him, I was in the bank when this man came over to me and said, "Excuse me, I hope you don't mind me asking but how is Philly?"

'I said to him, "You're talking about Philly Grimes, right?"

'He nodded, saying, "Aren't you Marie Grimes?"

'I said, "No, I'm Bridie Morrissey". He replied, apologetically, "God, wouldn't you think we'd know who's who at this hour of our lives?" He was exactly a year older than me when he died on his 60th birthday, the same day I turned 59.

'If you had Philly Grimes as a friend, you had a friend for life.

'Philly was a good one. One of the very best.'

Martin Óg still loves the game as much as ever, though he is not the greatest admirer of the modern game constructed by Limerick's John Kiely and others. While Tipperary of the 60s (below) are a team that Martin Óg loved playing against and watching as they delivered toughness and honesty on the field.

« CHAPTER 13 »

Family, Absent friends and Memories

Men of the Morrissey clan have played their part in almost every phase of the association's growth and development in this area. They have served two counties and many clubs down the years, but their loyalty and inherent allegiance to all that is best in the association is unquestioned.

– John Keane

I'VE A GREAT family.

They're into us most days and the girls regularly bring Brigid and myself out for spins, and no matter what I want to do, they'll always give me a hand doing it.

It's lovely to head out to Tramore with them, go down the Prom, get a cup of tea down there and then head home. I love the spins out around the county where I used to do the bit of shooting, and that jogs the memory well for me.

There's a lot of truth in the saying, 'It's good to be able' and I'm glad to be able to still do the things that put down the day for me. There's no substitute in the world for a good family and I should be very, very thankful that I have them alright.

The week after a match, my sons Frank and Eamon will go back through what we were after watching the previous weekend – who was good and who was bad and so on. I'm blessed to have the family I have… to have Brigid, the boys, including Martin who lives in Pleasant Prairie, Wisconsin, and my daughters Róisín and Niamh. They've all been so good to me over all these years. And of course, our daughter Helen, who left this world far too soon, is never, ever, far from my thoughts. The Lord have mercy on her.

Some traditions run deep. One of my grandchildren, Eoin, has a Harty Cup medal of his own from 2007 when De La Salle became the first Waterford school to lift the trophy since the Mount Sion team I captained won it in 1953. I was there that wet afternoon in Cashel when they beat St Flannan's and that was a very proud day for me.

Eoin works for the GAA now and he enjoys it enormously… he was a good soccer goalkeeper too. He's a great lad and his brother Oisín loves going to matches as well. It's nice to see the interest passing down the generations. Sure all the grandchildren – Dylan, Liam, Harri and Maebh – they all bring something different to the table. And to have two great grandchildren as well, Chole and Micheál.

My goodness, two more gifts.

I'm grateful for all of them.

◄ ◄ ◆ ▷ ►

Frank Morrissey

'BETWEEN MY GRANDFATHER and my father, as well as my mother's interest, there was no escaping hurling in our house growing up. I can remember heading off to matches on the bars of grandad's bike… and heading off with mam and dad in the back of the car. It was a way of life when we were young and it's gas the way some things stay with you.

'I remember one day when myself and Pat Ryan – 'Ryaner' – were going o cycling out as far as Dunhill, so we asked Brother Hickey who was in Mount S School at the time, if he'd like a few sloes. He said he'd love some, so we pic few bags while we were out there and brought them into him.

'Not too long after that, Brother Hickey handed me a bottle of sloe said, "Give that to your father"… so off I went home with the bottle and to the father. Mount Sion were playing Portlaw in a tournament fina and dad had the bottle drank by the time the match started. He thought since a Christian Brother was after making it, that it must have been non-alcoholic.

'That didn't turn out to be the case. The Portlaw team, despite them only living a few miles over the Suir from Piltown, were two hours late for the match; there was some church-related event going on, so all the while the Mount Sion were arseing around over in Piltown and they didn't know what to do with themselves.

'Even allowing for the delay for the throw-in, dad was still worse the wear when the match went ahead and Portlaw ended up winning. They must have God on their side following the Confraternity!

'I saw dad hurl more in Factory League matches than I did for Mount Sion and that was simply down to the passage of time. Myself and my mother went off in the car to see him play – and he'd have been in his early forties by then, playing at full-forward.

He was playing alongside Brendan Fennelly, who was one of the seven famous Fennelly brothers on the first great Ballyhale team. Believe it or not, Clover Meats played two Leinster finals on two successive Saturdays… one had been delayed from the previous year. Dad scored 1-4 in one match, and 4-1 in the other.

'I remember a woman standing near me during one of those matches and she was grinning at my father when he was stood over a 21-metre free… it was like listening to fingernails running down a blackboard, it went right through me. Dad flicked the ball too far ahead of him on the lift but even that didn't put him off. The ball bounced and landed on the ground; he struck it flat off the grass and ·ded up burying it in the back of the net.

'You're not laughing now,"' I said to her.

·e might have been something coarse added to that – my mother never ·ing bad language - but she bloody well deserved it. It was the last ·let out of her that day. I was 12, heading for 13, and all I was doing ·r the father.

·lay with dad once and that was the last match he ever played, ·r match against Butlerstown, if memory serves me. I was ·n 45 by then. I had the No 7 jersey thrown to me and ·the positions and threw the 14 shirt at someone.
·k my jersey off, flung it back at the selectors and ·ck. My father is better than him".

'My father said to me, "Put that jersey back on you!"'

'And I said back to him, "I won't… You're better than him and I'm not going out unless you're playing".

'"Put it on… I'm getting auld,"' dad ordered.

'So I did what I was told and played. We went well in the first-half despite playing up the hill in Portlaw and then we had the hill for the second-half, so we were well set up. I set off down the field and knocked the ball over the bar and shortly after that, my father was brought on at full-forward. The next ball came my way and the cry from the line was "Over the bar… over the bar". Well, I had only one thing in my head.

'I lobbed the ball into dad and he flicked it into the net.

'You could have taken me off after that. The rest of the match didn't mean anything to me. I made dad look good! And that was the only time we ever played together. It was some buzz. I didn't boast about it to anyone in school or anything like that, that wouldn't be my style at all. That was something for my father and myself. Now there was one other job I did for him on a more regular basis than supplying a ball into him to score… I used to be in on the sideline with him, with a pack of 20 Players cigarettes and a lighter in my pocket.

'And my job at half-time was to get out to the 13-metre line with the Players and lighter, and if I wasn't out there in double time, there'd have been hell to pay. Dad wasn't the only one… there were at least 10 players smoking Carrolls, Major, Players and so on.

'There'd be plumes of cigarette smoke before the change of ends… it can't have done my health much good in hindsight!'

◄ ◄ ◆ ▷ ►

WE ALL HAD to do our best to get through Covid.

It was a very tough time, but I know a lot of people had it a lot harder tha[n] did. While I wouldn't have been going to matches in the flesh if there'd bee[n] pandemic, I'd never miss a match on the television. And when all sport gro[und] a halt, there was a void in my life.

I missed the matches hugely, and that's the God's honest truth[.] hurling day and night if it was on the television. And of course we'd n[ot] knocking on the door then throughout it all… the children were great to us, but we all took the restrictions into account.

It wasn't easy but we got by in our own little 'bubble'.

Being at home the way we had to be during the pandemic got me thinking about things I used to do but don't do now. For years, I used to go to Tommy McLoughlin's – the Tavern Pub on the Lower Yellow Road - every Monday and there'd usually have been five or six of us who'd go in there for a cup of tea and a chat about hurling, politics and everything under the sun.

But that's done with now and I miss that a lot.

Three of the group from Tommy's – Tommy himself, Paddy Murphy ('Paddy Moremiles' as he was known all over town) and Jim Byrne – they're gone now, God rest the three of them. Tommy, even though he was running the pub, always sat down with us and enjoyed the chat.

I knew Tommy since my school days… he played with De La Salle. One day, we were talking about hurling and he brought up his days in De La Salle, when they beat Mount Sion in the semi-final of the Dean Ryan Cup. I remembered it well. We were winning up to the last minute and I was running to try and get to a ball and a De La Salle fella was holding onto me. I turned around and shouted at the ref.

He blew the whistle alright, but he gave the free against me… and didn't De La Salle score a goal off that free and it won the match for them. They lost the final about a month later. Tommy always maintained that we'd have won the final ve'd won that 'semi' instead. It must have been the only winner's medal I didn't v hands on.

' two old friends who lived just below me here… Denny Duggan and they were both born in Kilkenny but they married into Waterford de their homes here.

et up after matches too… in the summer time, you could be side Denny's house, having a chat about the match and the

ven 20 years, that'd do me.

◄◄◆►►

Róisín Morrissey

'GOING RIGHT BACK to when I was very young, I have great memories of going out around the county with dad and Frank. I tagged along and generally moaned while requesting to be put up on one of their shoulders. More often than not, my plea was answered. If nothing else, saying yes kept me quiet for a while.

'Now, dad and myself wouldn't have had a lot in common during my teenage years. I was into alternative music, experimenting with my hair colour, wearing Doc Martens and generally being a moody teenager. But as the years rolled by, that dynamic began to change, something I've been grateful for ever since.

'I was young when I was having Dylan, my eldest son and I was dreading telling my parents that I was pregnant But when I told dad, the first thing he said was, "Sure isn't that great, you might have a little hurler for me!" I can't tell anyone how much those words meant to me – and still do. A child brings a great amount of love into a home and that was certainly the case when it came to Dylan. Daddy was way more hands-on as a grandparent than he had been as our dad because he had more time to give by then – and of course he could hand the children back!

'Both mam and dad were exceptional to Dylan, which meant they were exceptional to me. I didn't drive at the time, so for years dad brought us to work and collected Dylan from school. He often got out of bed to collect myself and my sister Niamh after nights out in Tramore. He even used to light my fire so we'd have a warm house to come home to after work.

'The outside world sees Martin Óg the hurler and the part of him always lights up when he talks about those great days with Waterford and Mount Sion – he has never lost his enthusiasm for the game. But growing up and all the way through to this day, I've seen the side that means the most to us as his children... a warm, generous and loving dad who was always there for us. And he still is.'

◄◄◆►►

Martin Morrissey

'DAD IS SUCH an honourable man. Good natured, competitive, the hard-working man of the family and very funny. That good humour has kept him going and it's a quality we'd all be the better for having a bit more of in our daily lives.

'Grandad Morrissey worked at Strangman's Brewery, where Waterford Distillery now stands on Grattan Quay, just below Rice Bridge in the city. He later worked in Morris's coal yard and used to carry the coal on his back home to keep his family warm. He was still cycling to Mass into his eighties and was very dedicated in everything he did. Dad carried on a lot of those traditions and loved cycling himself until the time came to retire from that past-time as well.

'Nanny was and is still in my soul. I never saw her in bad humour. She loved us all so much and could make a meal any five-star restaurant would have been proud of.

'I remember dad carrying me on his shoulders after I skinned my knee... and shouting out encouragement during my own matches. He came into the school one year with the rest of the Mount Sion panel after one of their county championship wins. When the players visited my class, he strode over to my desk, ruffled my hair and tied my shoelaces. I ended up going to a lot of the training sessions with dad when he got into coaching and there was always something to learn.

'During an old timers match, which was fundraiser for a dialysis machine at Waterford Regional Hospital, I saw dad hit a free from all of 70 yards – the most beautiful hurling stroke I reckon I've ever seen – long, straight and low angled. It dropped like a rocket over the head of the player marking Frankie Walsh who swivelled and knocked it between the posts. All the lads playing that evening were past their prime but there was no denying their quality. Dad was part of an exceptional group and he's justly proud of being part of those great Waterford and Mount Sion teams.

'By the way, I practiced dad's free-taking technique and I reckon it took me three years before I even got close to what he could do!

'I loved going hunting with dad. We ended up seeing so much of our beautiful countryside on account of it and it was brilliant being in his company like that. We'd watch the nine o'clock news nearly every night and talk about what was going on in the world. Dad and mam have always been there for us and growing up, they couldn't have been more supportive than they were. We know just how lucky we are to have been raised by them.

'After my son Liam was born in the United States, mam and dad came over every year to make sure Liam knew them and that they in turn got to know him. He loves them very much and they put in the mileage to build that bond. That's the kind of people they are.

Family has always been the most important thing for both my mam and dad. The rest – even hurling in the greater scheme of things – represents the small stuff. Now dad mightn't say that to everybody, but the people who matter most have always known where his priorities lie – and we've benefited from that. I couldn't be more grateful.'

◄◄◆►►

Niamh Morrissey

'I PROBABLY HAD a slightly different relationship with my dad growing up when compared to my other siblings. He was 47 years old when I was born and Clover Meats closed when I was around four or five. Daddy had a couple of different jobs after that but he would have been around home a lot when I was a kid while mam was working between the house and in the Little Sisters of the Poor. A lot my early memories are of scooting off in the car with him, doing all the family staples – going to the supermarket, visiting aunts and uncles, going up to my nanny, going off with the dogs, all those trips to the beach in the summer... wherever we went, we had a good time. The Sunday spin was always a highlight. We all loved it.

'As I got older, when I'd be heading off into town, he'd be giving out about my short skirt. "Put your coat on", mam used to advise me before nights out, "your father won't bring you in otherwise". I'm 41 now and he still gives out to me about the length of my skirts!

'Mam and dad were always very good to us; they still do absolutely everything they can for us, even at this stage of their lives. And it's a pleasure now to be able to give something back to them and to mind them in their mid- to late-eighties. They're very good to myself, my husband Graham and our daughter Maebh and we love them dearly. We love bringing them off for spins, bringing them over for dinner and calling in home. To have them both around is something I'm so grateful for; it was something I worried about a lot when I was young since they were that bit older when they had me. But I'm so lucky to still have them in my life. We all are – and I'll never be able to thank them enough for all that they have done for me.'

◄◄◆►►

THERE'S NOT MUCH fun in getting old.

The slowing down is probably the hardest thing about it. It's a big effort now to get out for a walk, whereas before I used to leave the house here and I'd go out as far as Ballinaneeshagh, down the Witches Lane... across the Green Road, then onto the Tramore Road... and back up past the Regional Sports Centre and up by Kingsmeadow, alongside the old Glass Factory site... and back home.

During the summertime, there'd be blackberries and wild gooseberries to pick along the way. I loved that walk but I couldn't do that now... all in all, still, I'm very satisfied with the way I am. I really have no complaints, especially when I see other people my age suffering with all manner of diseases, be it Alzheimer's, other forms of dementia and so on. Thanks be to God, I haven't any of those things yet.

I'm glad that my mind is still pretty sharp and I've plenty of memories I can recall, be it matches I played in or matches I went to as a supporter.

Some matches just give you certain feelings and it's great to be able to recall so many of them all the while and then all the stories that went with them. And certain losses stick in the memory a bit deeper than all the games I won with Mount Sion and Waterford.

I remember after playing Cork one day, and as we were leaving the ground, didn't Christy Ring appear at the same time. He came over and started talking to me... only a few words, and then he headed off.

Phill Grimes was walking out behind me, tipped me on the shoulder and said, 'What do you have that we haven't'.

'Why?' I said back to him.

'No matter how many times we play Cork, Ringy always comes over to have a chat with you.' With a big smile, I told Philly, 'Ah, Christy knows who the boss is!'

And how we laughed.

I remember playing with Ring for Munster up in Castlebar in the Railway Cup. We travelled up on a Saturday and we were served up a mixed grill – steak, liver, the works – when Ring appeared at my shoulder.

'Don't you know today is a black fast?' he said.

And I said to Christy, 'Yes, I do… but our Bishop is a butcher and your Bishop – the two Bishops were related – is a fishmonger, so we in Waterford have permission to eat what we like!'

Then in 1959, the Railway Cup final was held over from St Patrick's Day until June 7 for the official opening of the Hogan Stand and we were playing Connacht. We stayed in Barry's the night before and Larry Guinan and myself came down to the dining room for breakfast and Guinan was wondering where we'd sit.

'Sure we'll sit down alongside the lad… Christy!' I said.

He was sitting on his own, so over we went.

Christy never spoke about anything else other than hurling, and he knew he was the best. So we're chatting away and then he said to me, 'Óg, ye'll win the All-Ireland this year.'

'Do you think so?'

Said Christy, 'Yes, I do. Sure who is going to beat you?'

'Kilkenny,' I suggested.

'No.'

'Wexford?'

'No.'

'Dublin?'

'No.'

'Tipperary?'

'No.'

'Limerick?'

'No.'

'Cork?'

'Sure, who have Cork?' he asked me.

'Well, ye have Mick Cashman in goal, Jimmy Brohan at corner-back…'

Then Christy interrupted me.

'I'll tell you the truth about Cork. We have two… John Lyons and myself, and Lyons is nearly bet.'

Ring called it. He was 39 years of age by then and he went out that day and scored 4-5 out of Munster's 7-11 in what was a comfortable win for us.

That October, he was named the Texaco Hurler of the Year.

Ringy was something else, the Lord have mercy on him. There's no one who compares to him given the way he played. He could hit the ball from any place and no one every really dominated him physically.

Christy was a perfectionist.

◄ ◄ ◆ ► ►

Phil Fanning

'ÓG RELISHED THE Railway Cup.

'He loved playing with the very best, so playing for Munster alongside Christy Ring and Jimmy Doyle, along with his Waterford teammates meant an awful lot to him.'

Frank Morrissey

'ANYONE WHO EVER said anything to me about being Martin Óg Morrissey's son when it came to my time hurling, it all went straight over my head. But if anyone kept at it with me, I had a standard reply.

'No, I won't be as good as him. I'll be better.'

'But that talk in general never really bothered me. I could only be the best that I could be, the same as anyone else playing any sport. Up to the age of 12, I played in the forward line.

'Then Johnny Walsh, a Shamrocks man who'd been a selector with Kilkenny, took on our team at Mount Sion (school) and we were up for trials for the Rice Cup team and he put me in at corner-back… and then the following year I was centre-back, which was where I played up to under-21 level, when things went awry due to injury.

'I got a belt when I was 18 – I was playing under-21 at 15 – and I was never really the same after that. At 23, I was told I had Ankylosing Spondylitis by Mick Molloy, the rugby doctor in Cork. And once he found out I was playing sport, he told me I had to give it up and take up something like swimming.

'It was the hardest thing anyone ever had to tell me and I lost all interest in hurling after that.

'I stopped going to matches entirely. I didn't want to be looking at fellas I'd played with and against. Sitting and standing for too long wasn't going to do me any favours either.

'So while going to hurling matches wasn't something I ever did much with dad after that, we went shooting together and brought off the dogs... and I did that with him from the age of 17 up until he finished up with all that.

'We both got a lot out of it and that it came along before my own years hurling ended was a blessing in disguise when I look back on it now. But I've always been happy to talk about hurling with dad – and having the shooting and the dogs was an added element for me.

'I still ring mam and dad after matches to talk about whatever game we might have been just after watching on television... it might only be for five minutes, but we've always had those chats.

'Hurling has definitely kept him going... my mother too for that matter.

'He loved playing and he loved his time training teams too, be it Mount Sion, Waterford, Glenmore, the Shamrocks, Mullinavat and Tullogher. Dad gave an awful lot to hurling and to do what he did with Glenmore was very special... that was something he drew a lot of pride from and so he should.'

◄ ◄ ◆ ▷ ►

HARD AND ALL as it's been to say goodbye to so many of the friends and hurlers I knew at all the funerals down through the years – and some of them far too soon like Ring and Philly Grimes - there's never been a shortage of good stories the day of a burial.

I've always enjoyed meeting fellas I played against years ago and having a good old chat with them, even allowing for the circumstances that have brought us together. At Jimmy Doyle's funeral, when 'Mackey' McKenna told me I was the best centre-half-back he ever played against – I'm only five foot eight – I felt about seven foot tall when he said that to me.

◄◄◆►►

Frank Morrissey

'ONE OF MY family jobs is to bring dad to the funerals and there's been a share of them over the years at this stage. I knew a good few of the 1959 players myself, Austin Flynn in particular. He was a lovely man. But you'd be after getting the first cup of tea after a burial when the greetings would really start in earnest.

'How are you doing, Martin'… and 'Óg, how's the form?'

'So, being the good chaperone that I am, I'd tell anyone saying hello to him, "I'll make it short for ye. He's deaf, the eyesight isn't great, the kidneys have seen better days, he has diabetes… but other than that, he's grand! And he'll tell you the very same himself when he leans into you".

'The contrariness has kept him going… that and the fact that there's a history of longevity on both sides of the family. But between himself and the mother, they've kept each other going for all these years. They're some pair, all the same.'

◄◄◆►►

I'VE A GREAT family and I've had many great friends over the course of my life, Lord have mercy on all of them gone before me. Talking about them helps, even years later. They might have left this earth but they're not gone.

They're still in the mind's eye and still in our stories.

Martin Óg and Brigid with their family (from left - Niamh, Martin, Eamon, Frank and Róisín) and celebrating their 60th wedding anniversary with their family (below).

« CHAPTER 14 »

Martin & Brigid

I FIRST MET Brigid O'Connor at the Savoy Cinema on Broad Street, which is now home to The Book Centre. If you go in and look at the huge back wall in there nowadays, you can clearly see where the screen used to be.

I remember the night we met very well.

Myself and Billy 'Bullsick' Flynn, an old pal of mine, were gone to the pictures – I can't remember what film was on – but I was sat alongside Brigid (pronounced Bríd but that's not how it is spelled) and started talking to her. And that's how it all began.

As the crow flies, we were only living about 200 yards apart so of course I knew of her from the time we'd have been going to school, but I didn't really get to know her until we said hello that night in the Savoy.

A priest called Father Farrell who ran the Confraternity of Christian Doctrine – part of the Catechism – was in Mount Sion one day and he said he wanted to see me the following Friday night over in the church.

He wanted to make me a prefect, which would mean I'd have to look after a couple of seats.

'And if you don't come down,' he warned, 'I'll set sceachs at the end of Morrison's Avenue.'

He knew very well that's where I used to stop to talk to Brigid!

◄◄◆▷►

Brigid Morrissey

'SIXTY-FOUR YEARS we are married.

'*Sixty-four years.*

'That's hard to credit when I stop to think about it, but then in another way it's gone by like the blink of an eye. And of course, we know each other a lot longer than even that. I'll go back to when I was 14 years of age, living on Morrisson's Avenue and by then I'd not given boys or boyfriends any kind of thought.

'I'd no interest whatsoever. All I wanted to do was to skip and play ball, wearing white ankle stockings... and my hair in a big satin bow. There was a girl in school called Helen Scanlon, who asked me to go up to the Sportsfield with her.

'Now, I used to always go and watch Mount Sion's hurling matches, but I didn't know who was who or what was what, but what I did love was the hurling itself.

' "Come up with me", said Helen.

' "There's a fella up there that I'm mad about."

'Ah go way, Helen, I don't want anything to do with any fellas', I said back, but that didn't stop here.

' "Ah, Brigid, will you come up with me, will you?"

'Anyway, up I went with her. The fella she was talking about was Martin... he'd played in the match and as he was coming out of the field, Helen said, ' "Brigid, there he is, there's the fella... I'm mad about him!"

'I said to Helen, "Ah now, Helen, sure he's gubby... he hasn't a tooth in his head".

'Martin was 17 by then. Helen might have had an eye on him... apparently, half the town was after him, but Martin and myself ended up together. And he's the only fella I ever went with. The children would tell you he idolises me and always has.

'I feel the very same way.

'There was one week when my mother, Kathleen O'Connor, was sick at home, God love her, and I was after minding her for the week. She knew I loved going to the pictures so she said to me, "Go down to the pictures, girl and enjoy the film". It was a matinee.

'So I went down to the Savoy and I put my cardigan on the back of the seat I sat on. The next thing was I got a tip on the shoulder and it was Martin… he was after seeing me before I saw him. He was after seeing me going down the Yellow Road on a bicycle. So he asked a girl called Mary Grant who I was with, to find out a bit more about me and what I was like.

'Anyway, my cardigan fell off the seat in the cinema and Martin picked it up, and said, "Miss, you're after dropping your cardigan" and he handed it to me. Then he looked at me, gave me a big smile and I said, "Thanks very much".

'Anyway, once the pictures were over, I ran out of the cinema. It wasn't that I was running away from him… by then I just had no interest in fellas, but they were running after me morning, noon and night all the same.

'The next time I took notice of Martin – or maybe it was the other way round – was up at a carnival at the Barracks. It was a fundraiser for the new Holy Family Church in 'New Ballybricken' as we locals used to call it. I was in a concert that was part of the carnival but when it was over, we were standing outside where the carnival had been on.

'I was wearing lipstick since I'd been taking part in the concert, when I got another tip on the shoulder. It was Martin, who was one of the 'bagmen' collecting money at the carnival that day. 'He said, "hello" to me and all I was thinking was why is this 'auld fella' saying hello to me. Before I said anything at all, he said to me, "I don't like that lipstick on you".

'Well who asked you?' I asked.

'Sure he replied, "I'll take it off you".

'I hadn't a clue what he was suggesting so I said back, "Buzz off, boy, I'll take it off myself" … and I walked off a little bit. But then Martin asked if he could walk me home that evening. And sure that was the start of it all. My sister Frances was with me as well and we came over 'The Hovel', the first turn to the right off Morrison's Avenue.

'When we got as far as there, when Frances was looking the other way, Martin gave me my first kiss.

'Our first kiss.'

‹‹◆››

BY THE TIME we got married in 1957, we'd been going out for about six years. By the standards of the time, we weren't in any real rush to get married. Sure why would we have been rushing?

We knew each other very well by the time we were married and we've had some time of it since over all the years. We found our own way to make things work between us and to look after our children, and I don't think we've done too badly. We've had highs and lows the same as everyone, but I think we reared our children well. The five of them are very good to us so we must have done something right between the two of us.

Hurling, inevitably, has been a significant part of our marriage, particularly in those early years together and onto my years training and coaching during the 70s and 80s. It was a big help that Brigid loved hurling – and Mount Sion in particular – long before we started going out together.

She'll tell you now that I'd still spend all day talking about it. Granted, she mightn't always be happy that hurling has been on my mind so much of the time for so much of the last 70 years!

‹‹◆››

Brigid Morrissey

'MARTIN USED TO wait for me outside school – the Mercy in Waterford – and it wasn't a big secret or anything like that. There was an auld rip of a nun I had teaching me who used to be going on about "some girls here going out with men".

'I knew it was me she was getting at but I did my best to pay no attention to that kind of talk. Martin used to meet me after school and he'd carry my schoolbag home for me. We used to go for walks around the town together when we were courting. You have to remember that I was one of eight sisters... I had no brothers; my mam lost two of them, the bed of heaven to them.

'So the only male company I had growing up with was my father Francey and the few boys I played games with out on the street. I wasn't used to being around any boy in and around my own age so it was a case of slowly but surely with

Martin. We started going to Mass and the Novena together – Martin was always holy – and I got used to being in his company.

'I wasn't left out in the evenings so my sister Kathleen and Martin… they always got on really well together, they used to go to the pictures. Now there were a few girls who used to say to me, "He's only with you because he wants to go with your sister" but it wasn't that at all. They were great pals and that was that, right up to the day she died.

'He repeated the last year in Mount Sion so he could play in the Harty Cup, but I kind of had enough of him for a while – we'd been going out for a time at that stage – and I asked him to just leave it be. Anyway, one day a cousin of mine, Peggy, asked me to come up to her house, around the corner from us and fix a frock for her… I've been a dressmaker most of my life.

'So up I went and who was there only Martin out in the kitchen. "Now", she said to me, "Ye're meant to be together". And sure he was after being brought up there under false pretences himself.

'Peggy used to make lovely chips and she asked him to pop in because she had a nice feed of chips for him. So she asked us to sort it out and get on with things. So we did and that was our only "wobble". I stopped telling him to buzz off and things started to click. By the time I was serving my time as a dressmaker, I got to go out in the evenings with Martin, even though my parents, lovely and all as they were, were very strict about the way we were with each other and how much time we spent together.

'We were walking up the Yellow Road one evening, not quite a year after we'd stated going together and who came around the corner only my mother and father. When I was home later that evening – and my parents were back by then as well – my mother said, "Brigid, bring Martin up to the house. I want to meet him". My parents knew Martin's parents… my father delivered coal locally, so that awareness was there.

'So when I brought him up, mammy thought the sun shone out of him and my father was the same. They were very fond of him and of course that was important to me. When I was 19 years old he said to me, "When will we get married?" We got our engagement ring in a shop down the town… I picked it out.

'Martin asked my father for my hand but I couldn't get married until I was 21… my father insisted on that.

'But I didn't mind, to be honest.

'I knew I was going to marry Martin anyway.'

◄ ◄ ◆ ► ►

Jim Greene

'BRIGID HAS LOVED the dirt under Martin Óg's nails all her life and still does today. She gives out about him because he won't wear his hearing aid, but she'd tell you he hears alright when he's called in for his dinner!

'She has idolised that man her whole life and he's the very same when it comes to her. Apart from being the hurler that he was, Óg was an extremely good looking man in his prime – and he knew it. But he only ever had eyes for Brigid.

'He's a great man and she's a brilliant woman. They've always been a wonderful couple. When my family went through tough times, the Morrisseys were always there for us. And I'll never forget that.'

◄ ◄ ◆ ► ►

THE WATERFORD NEWS noted our wedding on page 3 of the edition dated September 19, 1958. And here's what was printed:

MORRISSEY – O'CONNOR: The marriage took place at Ballybricken Church on Tuesday last between Mr Martin Óg Morrissey, Mount Sion Avenue and Miss Bridget O'Connor, daughter of Mr and Mrs Francis O'Connor, 21 Morrison's Ave, Waterford. Rev M O'Doherty CC, performed the ceremony with Nuptial Mass and Papal Blessing.

The bride, who was given away by her father, wore a full-length gown of white chantilly lace over slipper satin, with a full bridal veil. She carried a bouquet of pink roses. Mrs Mary Oag (sister of the bride) was matron of honour. She wore a ballet-length dress of lavender. The child attendant was Miss Ann Oag (niece of the bride). The best man was Mr Matthew Morrissey (brother of the groom).

Some 50 guests attended the reception in Dooley's Hotel after which the happy couple left on their honeymoon, which is being spent in Dublin and Wales.

The groom, who is a member of the staff of Messrs Clover Meats Ltd, is well-known in hurling circles. He usually plays centre half-back for Mount Sion, Waterford and Munster. The bride is a well-known dressmaker.

►◄◆►►

Brigid Morrissey

'WE GOT MARRIED on September 16, 1958 in Ballybricken Church and then we went on our honeymoon to Dublin. When I opened my case, confetti went all over our room… one of my cousins was after filling my case with confetti. So there we were, the two of us, down on our hands and knees picking up all the confetti!

'Then Martin said to me, "Brigid, I'm going to bed".

'I was terrified. I had no idea about anything like that.

'Then he said, "I won't go near you". To begin with, we lodged up in a house in Morrison's Avenue and those early years, at least for Martin, were all about hurling… sure he's still wrapped up in it. And I used to make his togs for him.

'And they used to be gleaming… he actually got the nickname "The Persil Kid" on account of how white they were. We'd no washing machine… everything was washed on the washboard and if you looked at any of the photographs of the teams Martin played on, his kit was always gleaming. His mother knitted his socks and I'd have his gear bag ready for him before training or a match.

'That was the done thing right from the start.

'He was never much of a man for pubs or drink. He always came home straight from training, which wasn't the done thing with a lot of the fellas he was hurling with. And he played squash as well to stay fit. He'd big strong legs under him and they served him well all the years he was playing hurling.

'But I never, ever interfered with his hurling.

'Sure Martin was even on the cigarette cards at the time, that's how well known he was… getting to go to New York and so on. I was delighted for his success and I knew how popular he was with people all over Waterford. But I was married to him and that was always enough for me.

'I was always proud of how Martin played and how good he was. He was a great hurler and he earned every honour that came his way.

'There was one evening I went up with Eamon in my arms to the Sportsfield when Martin was playing. I went up to the gate before the match and whoever was on it wouldn't let me in after he had just left in a family from the top of Morrison's Avenue… and they were all into soccer.

'Martin spotted me outside the gate and asked what I was doing out there and I told him that the fella on the gate wouldn't let me in. "And what the hell are they (the soccer-loving neighbours) doing over there?" Martin said for more than me to hear.

'Martin went up to the gate and I say he felt like throwing a punch on him, which he didn't, mind you. "Come here now," Martin said. "That's my wife and my baby. Now, you get out of the way and leave them into the field. If that crowd you just let in can sit over there, then my wife and baby can come in here too. How dare you stop them coming in."

'He lifted the fella at the gate out of it. I think certain people might have been a bit jealous of Martin and I really don't know why. I think what he did for so long out on the field and for how long he did it might have been a bit underappreciated. But not by anyone under this roof.

'Not ever. Martin has always had all of our backs and we've always had his.

'The two weeks after Waterford won the All-Ireland and I was at home after having Eamon, Martin's mother – not my mother – felt she had to say something to him because the players were the toast of everywhere they went, showing off the MacCarthy Cup. Sure he was caught up in the excitement of it all, which, looking back, was hardly surprising.

'One evening into the celebrations, nanny – that's what I always called her – says to him, "Where the hell were you? Your gallivanting days are over. You're married. You have a child and there's your wife. Don't ever put your foot inside the door again this late."

'And that was it… he never did that again. I got on great with nanny… I idolised her. I didn't mind it, though. I can't say I was mad at Martin or anything. Sure they were after winning the All-Ireland, after all.

'THE MORNING WE were getting married, I was going out the door at home when my mother said to me, "Now, Brigid, you're marrying Martin. And when

Martin comes home from work, don't have anyone in your kitchen. Do what I always did. Have your hair combed nice, a clean pinny (an apron) on you, your hair combed and your lipstick on… with a nice fire lighting and his dinner ready on the table for him".

'Then my father told me, "Brigid, Martin's hurling, as long as he's playing, is always going to come first". But all of that went in one ear and out the other. I never felt like one of these "hurling widows" or anything like that. I knew very well who I was marrying and what hurling meant to him.

'That was definitely one thing about married life I was fully prepared for before I took my vows.

'When Martin came in the door after a match, I knew the minute I'd see him if things had gone well or badly. And if he wanted to talk about it, I'd answer him. Now he never treated me any differently regardless of a result. I always understood him.

'I was big into hurling myself and always had been so we always got on well when it came to hurling too… my uncle Paddy O'Connor hurled for Waterford in the 40s, so I'd a good understanding of hurling when we were growing up.

'The year after Martin stopped playing senior hurling, Róisín was born. We'd just moved out of Mount Sion Avenue where Martin's mother lived and built the house that we've lived in ever since. It was like starting a new chapter for us, really. We'd not lived on our own as such since the first year or so that we were married so that was a huge thing for us.

'Looking back, I think it was good for all of us that there were other changes going on in Martin's life when his senior career with Mount Sion ended. But all the knowledge he built up over the years was never going to go to waste after he stopped playing so he was bound to end up training teams with Mount Sion, and then over the river in south Kilkenny, and he had great success over there as well.

'No player ever got worse after getting training or any advice from Martin. He knew his stuff… and he'd tell you himself that he still does!

'The two of us are at an age now where most of the people we knew best are lying in graveyards all over Waterford and beyond. The lads Martin played with for the club and with Waterford, sure he misses all of them, especially the Mount Sion lads who he knew that bit better, naturally enough.

'He loves looking back on things as he saw them… he's the first person in most of his own stories but sure that goes for a lot more than Martin, when you think about it. He had great respect for all of them, for Frankie Walsh, Mick Flan, Philly Grimes, Tom Cheasty and so on. He idolised Frankie and Tom.

'I always knew he was confident in himself, that he was someone who spoke his mind – and that hasn't changed at all over the years. He was always comfortable in his own skin and I accepted him for the man he was.

'Martin knew he was a good hurler. I did too. And I still do, 60-odd years later.'

◄◄◆►►

FOR THE BEST part of 70 years, Brigid has done some amount for myself and even more for the four children. We know we've a lot to be thankful for.

She's a good one, God bless her.

Martin Óg and Brigid, then and now... and surrounded by grandchildren and great-grandchild (standing from left: Eoin, Dylan and Oisin. Sitting from left: Brigid, Harri, Chloe, Meabh and Martin Óg).

« EPILOGUE »

Thoughts on a Happy Life

MY HEALTH HAS, by and large, served me well.

I do what the doctor tells me… the wife maybe not so much!

But I've got many a reminder of my good fortune over the years when I think of all the funerals I've been too, of fellas I went to school with, lads I worked with and the great men I hurled both with and against.

I've had more than one evening sat in the front room at home, surrounded by my medals and mementoes, thinking about a lot of them, especially during Covid when the handbrake went up, especially for people my age.

Births, deaths and marriages, all gone by in what feels like the click of a finger. The handful of us left since 1959… Mickey O'Connor, Jackie Condon, Larry Guinan, Taylor O'Brien… Brigid being with me for all these years and she of course being so lucky to have had me for all this time!

I hope there's a few years left in us yet, with the help of God.

To have the children, grandchildren and great grandchildren calling in the way they do to us, sure you can't put a price on that. I'm often sat out in the hall on a summer's day, enjoying the good weather with the front door open and I see them all coming in before they've even seen me.

I'm still in the box seat, after all these years. Sure you can't beat that.

I think not drinking to excess over the course of my life hasn't done me any harm. It's not that I'm averse to it but I never went too hard on it, and when I did drink I always had grub after it. But I never lost sight of how dangerous drink could be.

All the years cycling over and back to Clover Meats definitely built me up a bit too. Fresh air is the best tablet you could ever take and between cycling, the dogs, going shooting and hurling, I never lacked for that either.

Every day of the week, I used to have the hurley in my hand. Even it was only out on the road on Mount Sion Avenue, pucking the ball around with five or six lads, I always got something out of it. Shooting and bringing the dogs out certainly filled a gap after my playing days ended but nothing could ever replace hurling.

I'd still happily watch matches morning, noon and night.

I'm grateful that my father instilled a love of hurling in the whole lot of us from an early age. The game has been very good to me and I'm very glad of that now as I look back. The modern style of hurling mightn't be my cup of tea a lot of the time but all the while, there's still no sport that comes close to it.

It's our game and we've every right to be proud of it.

Now, someone might think *My Way* would be the Frank Sinatra song that first comes to mind when I think about my own life and all that's gone with it. But there's a bit of a chorus in another of his songs that came up when this book was being put together.

> *'Still in all I'm happy*
> *The reason is, you see*
> *Once in a while along the way*
> *Love's been good to me.'*

I've had a grand life and sure there's a bit of living to do all the while.
And a few more matches to talk about yet…

« BIBLIOGRAPHY »

Casey, Kevin ('Fifty Year All-Ireland', WLRfm, 2008)

Fullam, Brendan: *Off The Field and On: Triumphs and Trials of Gaelic Games* (*Wolfhound Press, 1999*)

Fitzpatrick, Regina *(GAA Oral History Project interview with Pat Fanning, November 21, 2008)*

King, Seamus J: *A History of Hurling [Second Edition] (Gill & MacMillan, 1998)*

McCarthy, Tomás: *Waterford Game of my Life* – Waterford's Greatest Hurlers remember the game that will live with them forever (Hero Books, 2021*)*

Mac Murchú, Irial: *Power: An Camáin (1994, Nemeton)*

O'Connor, Kieran (*'This Sporting Life: Michael O'Connor, WLRfm, 2022)*

O'Neill, Jack: *A Waterford Miscellany* (Rectory Press, 2004)

Smith, David: *The Unconquerable Keane – John Keane and the rise of Waterford Hurling* (David Smith, 2010)

Smith, Raymond: *The Hurling Immortals* (Bruce Spicer Ltd, 1969)

The Irish Examiner/Cork Examiner

The Irish Independent

The Irish Press

The Irish Times

The Munster Express

The Waterford News/Waterford News & Star

The Mount Sion Club Souvenir Record (1974)

www.mountsiongaa.ie

www.delasallegaa.ie

« APPENDICES »

1953 Harty Cup Final Match Reports

Note: It's clear from the reports below, given the common phraseology in both pieces, that both of Waterford City's local titles had a common source for their main match report details, hardly an uncommon practice in regional journalism either then or now. But the homecoming is subject to different comment from correspondents who were, one can only assume, on the ground as Mount Sion disembarked from the special train in Waterford with the Harty Cup. Both pieces are worth recording in the context of both Martin Óg's own story and the strides Waterford hurling would make at inter-county level before the end of that remarkable decade.

– Dermot Keyes

◄ ◄ ◆ ▷ ►

The Waterford News, March 27, 1953

Won Harty Cup for First Time

In Thurles Thriller

Mount Sion CBS 3-2
St Flannan's College 1-7

MOUNT SION CBS, Waterford, won the Dr Harty Cup (Munster Colleges senior hurling championship) for the first time in their history, when at Thurles on Sunday they defeated the holders, St Flannan's College, Ennis, by the narrowest of margins in a thrilling final.

The game ended in a welter of excitement as both teams fought for the decisive score. St Flannan's four points down with 10 minutes to go, rallied in traditional style to level the scores on the call of time. Lost time was being played when Matt Morrissey sent the ball high between the posts from a 21-yards free to give Mount Sion the all-important score for victory.

Mount Sion fully deserved success in a game which could have gone either way in those tense closing minutes. They had the tonic of a snap goal and inspired by this score they outplayed their opponents in most departments to lead 2-0 to 0-4 at the interval.

While St Flannan's had the advantage in height and physique, their defence did not play as well as in previous games (and) found it hard to cope with a fast and clever Mount Sion attack. The Waterford boys showed fine fighting qualities in (the) face of pressure and never allowed the holders to settle down to their usual game.

Mount Sion opened the scoring when P Walsh availed of a defensive slip to crash the ball home from close in. St Flannan's fought back for J Ryan to send over the bar from thirty yards. The Waterford boys were back again soon afterwards for J McGrath to send in a grand goal from the left corner.

Flannan's had the better of play towards the close of the half, Holohan and L Murphy (0-2) adding three but two points separating the sides at the interval. Points by L Murphy and P O'Malley on the resumption were countered by M Morrissey (0-1) and T Conlon (1-0) scoring for Mount Sion, who at this stage were four points ahead.

M Morrissey missed a free to Mount Sion before Flannan's had a goal in a melee. L Ryan followed with a point to level the scores. Morrissey's point in lost time gave Mount Sion victory.

His Grace, Most Rev Dr Kinane, presented the cup to the winning captain, M Morrissey, amidst scenes of great enthusiasm.

The GAA Notes and News column, also on page 8 of that week's edition, led off as follows:

CONGRATULATIONS to Cnoc Sion for their splendid victory over St Flannan's (Ennis) in the Harty Cup Final in Thurles. They brought that covered trophy to Waterford for the first time.

Conceding weight and height to their opponents, they used their speed to good advantage and heartened by an early goal held the margin throughout to win by a point margin, 3-2 to 1-7. An outstanding display by M Morrissey at centre-field and sterling defence work by Teehan, Walsh and Conlon gave St Flannan's little scope for scores, while Walsh, Power and Foley made good use of the opportunities to gain a hard-earned victory.

The large Cnoc Sion following (which travelled by special train) maintained a constant roar of applause and greeted every Cnoc Sion score with tremendous cheers.

Returning home, the players and supporters formed a large procession at the station and headed by their Flute Band marched to Cnoc Sion Schools.

◄◄◆►►

The Munster Express, March 27, 1953

Made Hurling History

Mount Sion win Dr Harty Cup for First Time

Thrilling Game at Thurles

Victory Secured by Minimum Margin

Mount Sion CBS (W'ford) 3-2
St Flannan's College (Ennis) 1-7

Mount Sion, Waterford, made hurling history at Thurles on Sunday last, when, after a thrill-packed game, they defeated St Flannan's College, Ennis (holders) by the minimum margin of a single point in the final of the Dr Harty Cup competition and brought this coveted trophy to our Suirside city for the first time.

WELTER OF EXCITEMENT

The game ended in a welter of excitement, as both teams fought for the decisive score. St Flannan's, four points down with 10 minutes to go, rallied in traditional style to level the scores on the call of time. Lost time was being played when Matt Morrissey sent the ball between the posts from a 21-yards free to give Mount Sion the all-important score for victory.

Mount Sion fully deserved success in a game which could have gone either way in those tense closing minutes. They had the tonic of a snap goal in the first five minutes, and, inspired by this score, they outplayed their opponents in most departments to lead 2-0 to 0-4 at the interval.

FAST AND CLEVER

While St Flannan's had the advantage in height and physique, their defence, which did not play as well as in previous games, found it hard to cope with a fast and clever Mount Sion attack. The Waterford boys showed fine fighting qualities in face of pressure, and never allowed the holders to settle down to their usual game.

THE SCORING

Mount Sion opened the scoring when P Walsh availed of a defensive slip to crash the ball home from close in. St Flannan's fought back for J Ryan to send over the bar from 30 yards. The Waterford boys were back again soon afterwards but J McGrath to send in a grand goal from the left corner.

St Flannan's had the better of the play towards the close of the first half. Holohan and L Murphy and P O'Malley, on the resumption for St Flannans, were countered by M Morrissey (0-1) and T Conlon (0-1) scoring for Mount Sion, who, at this stage, were four points ahead. M Morrissey missed a free to Mount Sion before Flannans had a goal in a melee. L Ryan followed with a point to level the scores. Morrissey's point in lost time gave Mt Sion victory.

His Grace Most Rev Dr Kinane, Archbishop of Cashel, presented the cup to winning captain M Morrissey amidst scenes of great enthusiasm.

WINNING TEAM

The members of the Mount Sion team were: J Goulding; F O'Brien, P Teehan, Seamus Power; Sean Power, M Morrissey, N Power; S Foley, B Ormonde; F Foley, T Conlon, T McGrath; F Walsh, T O'Mahony, P Walsh.

TUMULTUOUS RECEPTION IN WATERFORD

When the special train carrying the victorious team and over five hundred of their supporters, most of them juveniles, arrived back in Waterford on Sunday night, a big hosting of boys and adults was waiting at the North Railway Station to give them a tumultuous reception. For many minutes, the deafening cheering continued, and then a triumphal parade was marshalled into formation.

It was headed by the Mount Sion boys' flageolet band and, as it proceeded along the Quays, through Barronstrand St, Broad St, etc, to Bunker's Hill and Mount Sion, unbounded scenes of enthusiasm were witnessed. The captain, M Morrissey, carrying the cup on high, was 'chaired' by the youthful enthusiasts along the entire route, and, in every other respect, the parade was made as memorable as the historic occasion merited.

On arrival in Barrack Street, where the Mount Sion Schools are situated, Rev Bro Collins, in a brief address, congratulated the team on the victory and the people for their great reception to the boys. To commemorate the team's deserving win, the boys were given a holiday on Monday.

◄ ◄ ◆ ► ►

Irish Independent, October 5, 1959

Record Replay Crowd
Saw Waterford Win

Waterford 3-12
Kilkenny 1-10

Attendance: 77,285

Waterford supporters cheered with delight when the final whistle blew at Croke Park yesterday and the Decies men had won their second All-Ireland senior hurling title from a Kilkenny team that was glorious in defeat.

Croke Park was a picture of colour as a record replay crowd – 73,707 saw two very fit teams battle for the honours which were deservedly won by Waterford.

After trailing devastating Kilkenny for twenty minutes of the first half, Waterford shot into the lead with two fast goals and though closely chased by their opponents for a good part of the second half continued to play confidently and 10 minutes from the end there was no doubt about the ultimate result.

As their captain Frank Walsh stepped up on the dais on the Hogan Stand to receive the All-Ireland Cup from Dr JJ Stuart President of the Gaelic Athletic Association, and subsequently be presented to President de Valera, a storm of cheering broke over the ground.

Whatever may have happened during the game to mar things somewhat, when referee Gerry Fitzgerald from Limerick had to put a player from each side to the sideline, was forgotten.

Vanquished Kilkenny and victorious Waterford men embraced and congratulated one another wholeheartedly.

It was a sporting finish to a sporting game.

Streets Crowded

The acclamations of the Waterford supporters did not end at Croke Park. Last night they were still in victorious chanting moods in Dublin's streets, which during the day were almost impassible. So great was the congestion of vehicular traffic that extra gardaí had to be drafted to cope with the crowds.

Croke Park itself was a veritable sea of colour. The verdant pitch was a rich, lush green under a kind October sun.

The black and amber of Kilkenny contrasted with the blue and white of Waterford and, to a neutral observer, it seemed that the latter colours predominated.

The Artane Boys Band which led the parade in their colourful skirling dress, added to the pageantry of the occasion.

Not only was the attendance a record for a replay but it was also the only time on which the attendance for a replay was greater than for the drawn game.

If the game did not have all the thrills of the drawn game – this time there was no last second Kilkenny scores – it was equal to it in the cut, thrust and parry of two great teams. Waterford's forays led to scores and hard tackling was a sheer delight to watch.

If Waterford may be written down as the most popular All-Ireland winners for quite a while there is no doubt that the biggest cheer of the day was for the London and Antrim teams contesting the Junior All-Ireland final. London won, but Antrim had the sympathy of the crowd with them.

President de Valera was received at Croke Park by Mr Pádraig Ó Caoimh, General Secretary of the GAA and accompanied to his seat by the GAA President, Dr JJ Stuart. The attendance included the Taoiseach, Mr Lemass, the Minister for Industry and Commerce, Mr Lynch, the Minister for Defence, Mr Boland, the Minister for Posts and Telegraphs, Mr Hilliard, the Minister for Agriculture, Mr Smith, the Minister for the Gaeltacht, Mr Bartley, the Attorney General, Mr A O Caoimh, Mr Sean T O'Kelly and Mrs O'Kelly.

Most Rev Dr Kyne, Bishop of Meath, Very Rev Canon TB Walsh, PP Clonmel, representing the Bishop of Waterford and Lismore, Most Rev Dr Cohalan.

The American Ambassador Mr Scott McLeod, Messrs Richard Jones, Mayor of Waterford, Sean S Ó hUallacháin, Mayor of Kilkenny, Ald J Carew TD, Prof Liam Ó Buachalla, Cathaoirleach, An Seanad; Gen R Mulcahy TD, Mr W Cosgrave, Mr L Cosgrave TD and Mrs Cosgrave, S Ormonde TD, G Boland TD, W Norton TD, P O'Donnell TD and Dr CS Andrews, Chairman, CIE.

Celebrations in Waterford

There was great jubilation in Waterford among the stay-at-homes when the result of the final replay was announced over the radio. After the final whistle sounded many rushed into the streets, waving blue and white flags. Last night bonfire blazed in practically every street throughout the city and county.

It was only a rehearsal, however, for the big reception that is planned for to-night when the team returns in triumph with the McCarthy Cup.

A triumphal procession will accompany the team through the streets to the City Hall, where they will be accorded a civic reception by the Mayor, Ald R Jones and they will be guests of the owners at the Waterford opening performance of Chipperfield's Circus.

Reception for the Winners

A reception for the Waterford team in the Grand Hotel, Malahide, last night, was attended by Dr JJ Stuart, President of the GAA. The London hurling team which won the Junior All-Ireland hurling final were guests of the Waterford GAA on the occasion.

Dr Stuart, after congratulating the Waterford team, referred to the London hurlers' win and said it was a wonderful thing that the Irishmen who had emigrated had remained loyal to the traditional games of their country.

Very Rev B Canon Walsh, PP Clonmel, who represented the Bishop of Waterford and Lismore Most Rev Dr Cohalan, said Kilkenny had been worthy opponents of the Waterford team.

Mr P O'Keeffe, Secretary GAA, said the team deserved every tribute paid to them. Mr P Ó Fainín, Chairman, Waterford County Board, GAA, said he meant it as a tribute to Kilkenny when he said that it was Waterford's greatest day because they had defeated Kilkenny.

Mr M O'Donoghue, ex-President of the GAA, said it had been no small achievement for the hurlers of the Decies to come from practically nowhere and win the All-Ireland championship.

Mr Pádraig Ó Maoleathaigh, assistant hon treasurer, Waterfordmen's Association, said the team's victory would do much to put hurleys into the hands of the young boys of the county to whom they were now heroes.

Mr Jim Mullarkey, Chairman of the London Co. Board, congratulated the Waterford team and said for them it was a proud day that they had come to win a Junior All-Ireland Final.

At the conclusion, Mr P Phelan, Portlaw, Waterford, presented a statuette of a Waterford hurler, which he had made himself, to Frankie Walsh, the Waterford captain, for the team.

The attendance also included Gen Mulcahy, TD, Mr S Ormonde, TD and Mrs Ormonde, and D Goode, secretary, Waterford Co Board GAA.

Kilkenny Team Honoured

The Kilkenny team were entertained to a dinner by the Kilkenny Men's Association at the Honybrook Hotel, Clontarf. Dr Stuart, President of the GAA and Mr P O'Keeffe, Gen Sec, paid tributes to the display of the team. Mr Nicholas Purcell. Chairman of the Kilkenny Co Board, congratulated Waterford on their win and expressed the hope that Kilkenny would be back next year to win. Mr M White, President of the Kilkenny Men's Association, also spoke.

◄ ◄ ◆ ▷ ►

Irish Independent, October 5, 1959

Waterford Sweep To Second Title in Hurling Replay

Second-Half Mastery Too Much For Kilkenny

Waterford 3-12
Kilkenny 1-10

By John D Hickey

In an All-Ireland senior hurling final (replay) comprising two of the most fleeting half-hours that I can recall, such was my enjoyment of it all, Waterford scored a 3-12 to 1-10 victory over Kilkenny at Croke Park yesterday in summer-like conditions before 77,285 spectators.

When referee Gerry Fitzgerald sounded the half-time whistle it was hard to believe that so much incident had been packed into so short a spell and up to the last ten minutes, when Kilkenny had clearly shot their bolt, the thrills continued.

The speed of the exchanges, hail-marked by a spate of scoring in the first half obviously "found out" Kilkenny, and there was never any hone chat they would once again "steal" a title.

Although over the hour the match did not compare with the drawn game last month, it must surely have confounded those who for weeks have been asserting that replays always prove something of an anti-climax.

In the early stages. it looked as if Waterford would be swamped when they were 1-4 to 0-1 in arrears in the eleventh minute; although aided by a wind which even the most conservative hurling man would regard as worth four points over half-an-hour.

Set Them Alight

Then Waterford found inspiration in a great goal by Mick Flannelly, a score for which Tom Cheasty, a man who it seemed could not be deflected from his intention, could claim much of the credit. That score came in the thirteenth minute, and from that stage onwards Waterford looked likely winners, in spite of the fact that Kilkenny are noted for having won games which at one stage or another it looked that they were out of it.

The turning point, as I saw it, came in the first five minutes of the second half. Kilkenny were then well on top, but they shot wide on three occasions in that spell from advantageous positions.

Now as one looks back it is an inescapable conclusion that the losers were so taken out of their stride by Waterford's first half recovery that they were upset. Subsequent events bore out that theory, when the black and amber jerseyed brigade fell to pieces in the closing stages.

Took Their Chances

It is also highly significant that in that vital spell after the restart Waterford had only two raids worthy of the name, yet they recorded a point from each, one of them a wondrous score by Larry Guinan from far out on the right wing. Kilkenny's reputation for pulling chestnuts out of the fire kept the game alive, but in the end they were caught in a cauldron from which all their great hurling craft could not devise a means of escape.

They were well and truly beaten by a team of superior craftsmen whose greatest attribute on this occasion was their refusal to panic in the face of peril. Waterford started like a side possessed by the jitters, but they recovered admirably from their most inauspicious start and then, early in the second half, they hammered nails in the Kilkenny coffin when they showed how chances should be snapped up.

Vast Improvement

Through most of the first half and for twenty-five minutes of the second, Waterford were the more accomplished performers. They ran into balls with an assurance that proved they had *learned a world of hurling in the drawn game; the covering of the full-back was marvellous in comparison with the anxiety of that trio last month; and forwards Frank Walsh and Larry Guinan, who had disappointed in the drawn game left an indelible imprint on yesterday's clash.*

Never have I seen a man who more worthily fulfilled the role of captain than Walsh. This, without doubt, was his match as was borne out by his. colleagues who all through adopted a down-the-left policy that paid rich dividends.

I cannot recall an occasion on which he was beaten, not even when the ball mischievously fell 'away', from him as he essayed a point off a free. He hit it off the ground and sent it straight and true between the posts for a point.

Yet. great as was his part in a triumph that was joyously hailed by Waterford men, this was by no means a one-man victory. The full-back line of Joe Harney, Austin Flynn, who "covered" Billie Dwyer most devotedly, and John Barron were men transformed from the drawn game.

Players Sent Off

Barron, with Dick Carroll of Kilkenny, received marching orders near the end of the third quarter following the only untoward incident of the game which, in my opinion, was caused by another player whose conduct escaped the vigilance of the referee who did not seem as alert as in the drawn test between the sides.

Martin Óg Morrissey also played a 'whale' of a game as he in turn blotted Mick Fleming, Dick Carroll and Tommy O'Connell. Mick Flannelly, Tom Cheasty and Larry Guinan also won honours in the hour, and while midfielder Seamus Power may not have been as prominent as Sean Clohosey in that area, the Waterford man hit as many telling blows as the man who opposed him through most of the game.

Jackie Condon, after a nightmare start, made a brilliant recovery, and Mick Lacey, at half-back, and at midfield up to the time of his injury early in the second half, carried his hurley with distinction.

Ned Power, in goal, now protected as a goalkeeper should be, and not " unsighted" by his backs, lived up to his Munster rating, and even if Phil Grimes, Tom Cunningham and John Kiely did not reap the expected harvest, they all contributed their share to a great victory.

Captains' Parts

If Frankie Walsh set his comrades-in-arms a grand example, so too, did Kilkenny's captain, Sean Clohosey, who gave a superlative display when switched to midfield just at the end of the first quarter. Kilkenny folk who cannot face up to facts – and such are to be found in every county – may claim that the story would have been different had they not lined out without Mick Brophy, a recent victim of tonsillitis, and had not Johnny McGovern, who received a collar bone fracture in the drawn game, been forced to retire after a quarter of an hour. But such was the fighting spirit of Waterford yesterday that I am convinced that excuses are unacceptable in this instance.

Only man in the losing side to compare with Clohosey was left full-back, John Maher, who hurled his heart out in an effort to repulse the Waterford tidal waves. Tom Walsh, Jim Walsh, Mickey Walsh and Billie Dwyer also battled most courageously all through, but their bravery and skill could not offset the shortcomings of many of their team-mates once Waterford found their feet.

Ollie Walsh, in the losers' goal, brought off a couple of capital saves, but was not the man we saw in the drawn game.

◄◄◆►►

Waterford's Finest Team

A chapter from '*The Hurling Immortals*' by Raymond Smith (First Published in 1969)

Note: Raymond Smith (January 1932 to April 2000) established a new standard in the coverage of Gaelic Games during the 1960s via the sports pages of the Irish Independent. The Thurles native also penned a host of outstanding books, including *The Hurling Immortals*, a book gifted to me my Grandfather Terry O'Hara (June 1922 to February 2007), a work I have frequently turned to during my career.

In 2004, Raymond's wife Sheila kindly gave me permission to run an excerpt from another of his books, A Century of Gaelic Games, in a Munster Final Supplement, which *The Munster Express* also featured in its 2015 Munster Final Supplement.

I felt I could not work on Martin Óg's book without featuring Raymond's observations on Waterford's greatest ever hurling team. Just as the Waterford team of the 1957-63 period defined inter-county hurling from the perspective of Déise supporters the world over, Smith's literary approach to his trade stands alone and I for one am grateful for his influence. Sportswriters are, in general, not remembered nearly as well as their medal-winning subjects. But the work of Raymond Smith and his contribution to the coverage and promotion of our national games should never be forgotten.

– Dermot Keyes

EARLY on in the 1957 championship campaign John Keane, trainer of the Waterford team, did not think that his inexperienced side would reach the All-Ireland Final. But they did – only to lose it, however, through over-anxiety at the crucial moment.

'What won it for us in 1959 was the loss of the 1957 crown,' said John Keane. 'The 1957 defeat made our players more steady and they did not make the same mistake twice.'

'I always maintain that we should have won that 1957 final,' said John Barron. 'The team was hurling with great fluency, particularly Seamus Power and Philly Grimes and it was a big shock when Kilkenny got there by a point.'

Kilkenny, in the opinion of John Barron, struck at the psychological moment – when Waterford thought they had done enough to win. John Keane advanced the theory that any young team no matter how good, going into an All-Ireland for the first time more often than not suffers defeat.

Seamus Power's reaction when it was all over was one of 'complete and utter amazement that we had lost'. One can well understand why Seamus would have felt like this. Ten minutes from the end Waterford were two goals up and seemed to have a firm grip on the game. 'Then in the space of five or six minutes the whole thing changed', said Seamus Power, 'and from being six points in front we found ourselves a point behind'.

There was less than a minute to go when marksman Philly Grimes, who had already that afternoon scored one goal and six points from frees, came up to take the all-important free on the Hogan Stand at the Railway end. Philly wanted to make certain that the ball would not deviate an inch from a true line – so he tried to lob it just over the bar. His puck fell short and Ollie Walsh saved. There was a hop ball in front of the Kilkenny goal followed by a nerve-wracking battle in the goalmouth. Waterford sent wide – and Kilkenny had won the title.

Seamus Power, John Barron and Martin Óg Morrissey all agree that it was inexperience more than anything else that lost Waterford the 1957 All-Ireland. 'If Tipperary or Cork had been in the same position,' said Martin Óg, 'they would have played it closed and held on to the two goals lead. We made the mistake of continuing to play an all-out attacking game.'

It was a very good Kilkenny team that beat Waterford in that 1957 final as they proved by their magnificent showing against Tipperary in the 1958 semi-final (a game I consider they might have won if luck had been with them in the first half), and the backbone of the 1957 team only failed to Waterford after a replay in 1959.

Fronting Ollie Walsh was perhaps the best full-back line Kilkenny produced in the fifties and sixties – Tom Walsh, Jim ('Link') Walsh and John Maher. Ollie Walsh himself will tell you that it was the best he played behind and pays tribute to the wonderful covering this trio gave him in the 1957 All-Ireland, when he first made his mark in a big way.

Flanking Mickey Walsh in the 1957 final were Paddy Buggy and Johnny McGovern, class on one side, outstanding courage, determination and enthusiasm on the other.

Mick Brophy and John Sutton formed a fine midfield partnership on that 1957 team; Mick Kenny, who won a junior All-Ireland medal with Tipperary, was at centre-forward flanked by the stylish Denis Heaslip and the captain Mickey Kelly. The full-forward line was an ideal set-up, Billy Dwyer providing the drive, Dick Rockett the opportunism and Sean Clohosey the polish and skill.

By 1959 Sean Clohosey was captain, Ollie Walsh was established in goal with practically the same defence in front of him, and changes in attack brought in Mick Fleming, Dick Carroll and Tom O'Connell. But most of the big names of the 1957 team formed the nucleus of the 1958 and 1959 sides.

There was an eleven year span between Waterford's All-Ireland triumph in 1948 and the 1959 success.

Seamus Power expressed the opinion to me that the Waterford style combined much of what was the best in Kilkenny and Munster hurling. The pattern of play was seen at its best in sweeping wing-to-wing movements.

It reached its peak of perfection in the swamping of Tipperary by 9-3 to 3-4 in the semi-final of the Munster championship in Cork in July 12, 1959 before a crowd of 27,236. It was all over at half-time, Waterford leading 8-2 to nil. Larry Guinan got three goals and Charlie Ware two.

The half line of Mick Flannelly, Tom Cheasty and Frankie Walsh was the key penetrating hub of the Waterford side. They showed tremendous pace and elan when in full cry.

It was a glorious and exhilarating sight to watch Tom Cheasty, a most unorthodox hurler, cutting through the centre, going right in maybe with the ball in his left hand and palming it over the bar; or having drawn the centre-back he would flash passes to Flannelly or Walsh who fanned out, thus stretching the defence to the very limit.

Inside, grey-haired full-forward John Kiely, a bundle of fire and energy, inter-changed positions with Tom Cunningham to upset further the opposing backs while Larry Guinan fitted perfectly into the scheme of things.

In 1959 everything went right for Waterford and they were undoubtedly the finest team in the championship. They beat the best in the country, overwhelming Galway and Tipperary and then mastered Cork in the Munster final.

They played a memorable drawn match with Kilkenny in the All-Ireland final on September 6, before an attendance of 73,707. Five points clear at half-time (0-9 to 1-1) they quickly stretched it to six on the turnover with a point by the dashing Tom Cheasty, who in this half too beat five tackles in one solo run of fifty yards before lofting the ball over the bar.

Two goals by 19-years-old Tommy O'Connell in a sweeping Kilkenny rally brought the teams level (0-12 to 3-3) – and the spectators to their feet. The cheering was continuous from that to the end.

Waterford again went four points clear through Tom Cheasty (2), Phil Grimes and Frankie Walsh (frees) and then, with Ned Power impeded by his own backs, a long ball by Paddy Kelly went all the way to the net.

Phil Grimes made the lead two points and time was ebbing away. Kilkenny swept back to make the lead with less than two minutes to go, a "70" by Mick Walsh being rounded off for a goal by Dick Carroll, who added two points, one from a solo run and one from a free.

Waterford made one last onslaught and a low ball from Seamus Power which Ollie Walsh seemed to have covered, was deflected to the net by one of the backs in trying to clear. Just on time Power with a raking puck from midfield was narrowly wide of the mark – but a draw was the fairest result.

Waterford gave Kilkenny a six-points start in the replay on October 4 and yet beat them in the end by eight points (3-12 to 1-10).

And then it happened. After a fine inter-passing movement, inspired by Tom Cheasty, Mick Flannelly found the net and immediately Waterford were a different side. Two more goals were to follow, one from Tom Cunningham, who connected brilliantly on an overhead ball, and the other from Tom Cheasty.

Frankie Walsh was undoubtedly, the man of the match. No captain could have accomplished more in inspiring his men to victory.

The Waterford full-back line did its job well. They did not fall back on their goalie but kept the Kilkenny full-forward line went out from Ned Power with the result that he conceded only one goal. Waterford had learned the mistakes of the drawn game.

And Waterford won despite any marked superiority at midfield where Sean Clohosey played very well for Kilkenny when he moved there at the end of the first quarter. Two players were sent off in the second half.

In 1957, they had beaten Cork by 1-11 to 1-6 at Thurles before 40,847 in the Munster Final. And again in 1959. Hero of the 1959 Munster Final, which Waterford won by 3-9 to 2-9, was right-full Joe Harney, who came off best in his duel with Christy Ring.

Partnering Joe Harney in the full-back line were Austin Flynn, a sturdy and reliable full-back and fair-haired John Barron, both honoured by Munster as was Martin Óg Morrissey the following season. Martin Óg Morrissey's flankers in the All-Ireland were Mick Lacey and Joe Condon and with Seamus Power and Phil Grimes providing the perfect balance at midfield there was an ample surge of power from defence through the centre to give the speedy attack all the changes it needed.

There was something in John Barron's hurling when he was at peak form that impelled attention. I have seen him in Thurles, against Cork in the championship coming through from his own goal-line almost to midfield, controlling the ball beautifully with the stick and to me on such occasions he epitomised quality and class. Like Jimmy Brohan of Cork, he could do wonderful things to delight the eye. In the long run, however, men who play it close can be far more successful and concede fewer scores , but they are not the same adornment to the game. The classic defenders are few.

Barron showed his natural hurling ability by playing at full-forward later in his career, but he will tell you himself, that he was never at home in the position. His best displays, as in the 1957 Munster final against Cork, at Thurles, were given at corner-back.

Martin Óg Morrissey was a hurler too in the true sense. He had his ups and down, but when he really struck form he could be great and his courage was never doubted. He had the distinction of leading Mount Sion to victory in the Dr Harty Cup in 1953 when they beat St Flannan's, Ennis, the previous year's winners, in the final.

Seamus Power's inter-county career began in 1949, but it was in 1957 that he became a star. He started at left-wing in the All-Ireland final against Denis Heaslip – it was the first time he had ever played in the back-line – but after twenty minutes he switched to midfield. He became best known as a midfielder though in 1965 he played in the full line of attack with Phil Grimes and Mick Flannelly.

The Seamus Power-Philly Grimes midfield partnership was, to my mind, as strong a pairing as has ever represented any county. Grimes brought style and class to everything he did on the hurling field.

The Mount Sion man made a notable contribution to Waterford's Munster championship win in 1948 and fifteen years later he was a match-winner against Tipperary in the National League (Home) final at Croke Park. Few could play John Doyle better.

We saw the last glorious flourish of the Waterford 1957-'64 side in the National League (Home) final against Tipperary in Croke Park, on May 5, 1963.

Even though they went on to win Munster honours that season and had another exciting battle with Kilkenny in the All-Ireland, I like to recall the day in May as the day when they proved beyond all doubt all doubt that they deserved a proud place indeed in the annals of Waterford hurling – and in the history of the game.

The first half was like the quiet opening of a symphony that reaches a stirring climax. We did not know what was in store for us. Tipperary led by 2-6 to 0-6 at half-time.

The second half was only a few minutes old when Roger Mounsey in the Tipperary goal fumbled a ground shot and Phil Grimes goaled. In a few bewildering minutes the game was transformed and Waterford had shot into a two points lead.

Then in the nineteenth minute came the moment of balance. Tipperary, desperately needing a goal to stem the tide, stormed to the attack; Donie Nealon centred beautifully to Jimmy Doyle, who found the net in spectacular style. Within a minute John McLoughlin had another.

Waterford had suffered two body blows. There were those who maintained that when headed they would collapse.

Four points down and only 10 minutes left! This time they did not falter. With high speed, scientific hurling that was a joy to watch Waterford rose to the challenge. Phil Grimes sent over the bar and then Mounsey fumbled for the second time and six Waterford attackers were in like tigers to rush the ball home.

Jimmy Doyle put Tipperary ahead with a point. But Phil Grimes had the balancing point and only three minutes remained.

Waterford swept through for two flashing points from Seamus Power and Phil Grimes and no-one could deny that their victory (2-15 to 4-7) was well-deserved.

'The team that beats Waterford will win the All-Ireland', said a man behind me in the stand.

And subsequent events were to prove him right.

◄ ◄ ◆ ► ►

Laying Decies ghosts to rest

By Dermot Keyes

(Irish Independent Sports Monthly, June 29, 2002)

IT'S been a while. The Beatles released their first LP, a young President was slain in Dallas and Noel Cantwell paraded the FA Cup around Wembley. And a team in starched white jerseys from the county of Waterford strode onto the Croke Park turf as Munster hurling champions. Oh yeah, it's been a while.

The Deisemen will end another 39-year wait when they emerge from the bowels of the Cusack Stand in 13 days' time for the first of this year's All-Ireland hurling semi-finals, just 70 minutes away from the fixture that a generation of ash wielders from Ardmore to Ballygunner have dreamt of, but not fulfilled.

Provincial champions at long last and one trophy relievingly secured, Justin McCarthy's side will hope to lay another ghost to rest in the All-Ireland series.

Waterford last won as Munster champions outside their southern confines in 1959, when Frankie Walsh became the first hurling skipper to receive the Liam MacCarthy Cup in the newly constructed Hogan Stand after defeating Kilkenny.

'I didn't think it would be as long as this between Munster titles,' said Pat Fanning, then County Board secretary, team selector and later to serve as President of the GAA.

'You have to remember, a number of players from the '63 team retired after that final, and had formed the core of the team which had won Munster championships in '57, '59, '63 and the All-Ireland in '59 of course.'

Four years later, with Galway tucked away in the Munster championship and no All-Ireland semi-finals on the calendar since 1958, Waterford's three-point win over Tipperary in the provincial decider at Limerick ensured a Dublin date for the Deise for the first Sunday in September.

Waterford boasted a wealth of experience with no less than 10 survivors from the 1959 All-Ireland victory over Kilkenny, who once again provided the final opponents in 1963.

Back in '59, a fresh from the minors Eddie Keher was listed in Kilkenny's half-forward line for his first appearance in hurling's showpiece. By the 1963 final, Keher was establishing himself as one of the sport's supreme stylists, a status he would reinforce with a set ball salvo against the Munster champions.

The pundits of those hot metal days had tipped Waterford to claim a third All-Ireland crown. As John D Hickey wrote in his match report for the Irish Independent, Kilkenny had been 'scarcely given a chance outside the confines of their own county'. Waterford, favourites in an All-Ireland It's been a while alright.

Hurlers of the stature of Philly Grimes, Austin Flynn, Tom Cheasty and Frankie Walsh, to name but a few, were the names with the Hartleys, McGraths, Brownes and a generation before them had grown accustomed to, sporting monkeys on the backs of 38 successive Deise captains who never lifted a pot between them.

'We'd been there three times as winners of the Munster championship and I thought after '63 that we might need eight, maybe 10 years before we might challenge again,' said Tom Cheasty, who operated as part of Waterford's feared half-forward line that summer. "I didn't think we'd have to wait so long to win a Munster title again.

'In 1963, we'd won the Munster, we'd won the League and we'd won the Oireachtas the year before, which was a fairly important competition at that time. We lost the All-Ireland final, yet we scored six goals. You have to remember it was only a 60 minute game back then so to score so well and still lose was disappointing from our point of view.'

Six goals. What team scores six goals (and eight points to boot) and loses an All-Ireland final? Waterford, only Waterford. Even their hard luck stories make the best hard luck stories.

Well, not quite. Only one other team has netted a half dozen goals and made the long trip home without Liam MacCarthy in the history of the game (for those anoraks among us, the dubious honour first fell to Limerick [Castleconnell] who scored 6-2 to Wexford's [Castlebridge] 7-0 back in 1910).

'It was a high scoring game,' recalled Waterford County Secretary Seamus Grant, the longest serving office holder in the country, 'the sort of score that would have won nearly any game. The match was in the balance right up to the finish. It was another milestone for Waterford, but not the sort of one you like to remember.'

Milestones were two a brass farthing that day on the Croke Park scoreboard, as goals and points flew over and under crossbar in a manner which to that juncture had never before been witnessed in almost eight decades of All-Ireland final action.

'Imagine scoring 6-8 and not winning,' said Frankie Walsh, a member of the team which reached three deciders in 1957, '59 (when he captained the victorious Waterford) and '63.

"It was an incredible match."

A record tally of scoring opportunities were created, 35 in all, not that any but the prophetic among the 73,000-plus attendance could have foreseen such a deluge, especially after the opening six minutes, when just three scores had been registered.

But a deluge of a different kind from the thunder and lightning final 24 years previously was about to open upon the sacred sod.

By the 13th minute, the pre-match omens appeared as good as their printed word, as Waterford led by five points and were good value for their lead.

However, as is customary with any reputable sporting drama, the tide of the game turned on two key moments within three minutes of the first half.

A probing high ball was lashed from distance towards the upright of Waterford goalkeeper Ned Power, who dashed from his goal line to meet the incoming sliothar. Power successfully connected with the ball, but unsuccessfully cleared the effort no further than into the grateful path of Tom Walsh, who slammed the ball home to cut the margin to just two points.

No sooner had Power taken the subsequent restart when he made another error which would prove the game's decisive name on the trophy moment. Sensing blood in the water, Kilkenny regained possession from Power's subsequent puck-out, channelling the ball into the palm of wing-forward Tom Murphy, who struck towards goal with a meeker effort than he would have wished.

Imagine his surprise when Power, perhaps a little punch drunk from his previous contribution to proceedings, allowed the ball to run across him, believing it destined to rest in the mesh in front of Hill 16.

Only it didn't. Murphy's shot bounced against the upright and into the onion sack. Power lashed his hurl into the turf in frustration. Kilkenny regained the lead, an advantage they would not relinquish.

'Ned thought the ball was going wide and let it go, but it came off the post and went in,' said team mate Frankie Walsh. 'Percy Flynn came on for Ned in the second half, we made changes in the back line and the half forward line. But our full-forward line that day was just superb. Seamus Power scored three goals, and he'd been in bed all week before that with the flu. The man I marked that day, Seamus Cleere, won man of the match and he deserved it. He'd a great game and that was no surprise as he was a great player.'

Though Kilkenny, largely through the free-taking accuracy of Eddie Keher, and some stout hearted defending from their magnificent half-back line of Cleere, Ted Carroll and

Martin Coogan remained ahead, Waterford's goal poaching kept them in the tie as the final moments approached.

In the second half alone, Waterford rifled home five goals to keep them in the game and had it not been for some custodial acrobatics from Ollie Walsh, the Deisemen could have ended with seven or even eight goals, which would surely have been enough to secure victory.

Both the flu-ridden Power and substitute John Meaney were denied by the bold Ollie as the clock approached 60 minutes with Kilkenny gamely maintaining a two-point advantage.

Victory was sealed by Eddie Keher's 10th converted free of the game, his 14th in all, proceeded by referee Jim Hatton's final whistle. For Kilkenny, a 15th title was secured. For Waterford, one more might have been during its golden era of hurling was added to. Waterfordians have long cursed those 'what ifs'. They've had more of them than most.

It's not often that a team which won an All-Ireland title, three Munster championships, a National League and an Oireachtas title in a seven-year spell is considered as one of hurling's great underachievers. But its All-Ireland winning captain disagrees with any such claims.

'I wouldn't think that way at all about that team,' said Frankie Walsh. 'You have to remember that there were lots of great sides around at the time...It's often been said to me by different people from around the country that that Waterford team should have won more, that we should have won three or four All-Irelands. And maybe we should have.

'I always thought that '57 and '63 were the ones we should have won. In '59, I thought we'd played very well in the first match but didn't play as well in the replay and won. And when you win an All-Ireland by eight points I don't think any of us were about to start complaining about how we'd played. We just had the bit of luck we needed that day to win.

'We had some great games with Cork and Tipp during those years. Kilkenny and Wexford were very strong, sure Wexford had a great side at the time. The standard was very high and very level across a few counties.

'Sean Clohosey came down to speak at the team's 25th anniversary in 1984 and said had he got the chance to play for any team it would have been the Waterford team of 1959, which was as good a compliment as could be made about that team.'

Pat Fanning has seen Waterford hurlers in action over eight different decades ('I can remember more than most about Waterford's better days, back when I was a youngster in 1931.') and feels the same sense of adventure about today's team as he did four decades ago.

'There is a great similarity in the way that both teams play the game. Their first touch, their movement off the ball and their use of the entire field is what made the team in '59 such a joy to watch. After this year's performance in Cork, it's great to feel justified in making the same comments about a Waterford team in the modern era.'

But a note of caution was provided by the former GAA president. 'But before we begin to really compare the team of today with the team of that era, they have got to go and win three Munsters and an All-Ireland first.'

Keeping feet in white and blue socks firmly on terra firma between now and August 11 is paramount, agreed both Fanning and Frankie Walsh.

"It's terribly important that this is done," Fanning added. "The Munster championship is over and done with and this is the beginning of a new competition. I'd imagine this is something that Justin McCarthy has been hammering into the players since the Munster final."

Walsh shared his former selector's sentiments. 'The lads played tremendously well against Tipperary; I think awesome best describes the way Waterford played in the Munster final. I'm not one for comparing teams or anything like that, but the best thing about the current team is the real sense of team spirit among the players. There's a great togetherness about the team and that can only help them when they play.

'There'd be no-one in the country bar the county they might end up playing in the final who would begrudge Waterford the All-Ireland, but there's a lot of hurling that has to be played between now and the final and we'll have to take whatever we can get.'

Tom Cheasty feels echoes of the 1995 championship in Waterford's run to the All-Ireland series and the fillip it could create for those hurling outfits from the perceived 'lesser' counties were Fergal Hartley and his team mates to prevail come September.

'It would be a great thing for the game if Waterford could go on and win the All-Ireland this year. The game needs it and I don't think there's anyone even in the big counties who would disagree with that.

'It was a great day for the game when Clare came through in '95 and it would be just as special to see Waterford win the All-Ireland after all these years.'

'It's lovely to have the Munster championship, but we're only halfway there,' said Frankie Walsh, hoping that Fergal Hartley can bridge the 44 years that separate his holding the Liam MacCarthy Cup with what he hopes will be a Waterford set of hands holding the trophy in September.

'I can't say anything other than that I was a very lucky person to be captain in 1959 and I've always considered myself to be lucky...my wife was up in Knock a few weeks ago saying prayers for the team, so let's hope things can work out. But it's lovely to be still involved.'

Lovely feelings come with these rare Munster championships down Waterford way. They haven't been Munster champions for, well, there's one tag no longer associated with *the men whose polyester jerseys are all the lighter than what the chain mail of history had lumbered them with for so long. Waterford as All-Ireland champions? It's been a while.*

Postscript: Waterford lost the 2002 All-Ireland semi-final to Clare by 1-16 to 1-13, with Kilkenny defeating the Banner in the final by 2-20 to 0-19. Since 2002, Waterford won Munster Senior Hurling titles in 2004, '07 and '10, National Hurling Leagues in 2007, '15 and '22, while losing All-Ireland finals in 2008, '17 and '20. My 2002 interviewees were Pat Fanning (1918-2010), Tom Cheasty (1934-2007), Seamus Grant (1931-2009) and Frankie Walsh (1936-2012). The time they gave me at the outset of my career in journalism meant a great deal then. Two decades later, it means a great deal more.

◄◄◆►►

The Munster Express, August 29, 2017

When We Were Kings

By Dermot Keyes

'RINGY? He'd have taken any backline in any generation to the cleaners,' Martin Óg Morrissey reminisced in his sitting room, just off Hennessy's Road on Sunday last.

Referencing Val Dorgan's seminal work of the great man from Cloyne brought the greatest of all time into conversation. Eddie Keher and John Doyle had already been referenced by Martin Óg, one of the few Waterford hurlers who has won practically every honour in the game, from Harty Cup right up to Liam MacCarthy.

'Christy was a gentleman and we became good friends after our days hurling were done with," said the Mount Sion legend (83).

'Whenever we'd be at a match, he had the knack of picking me out in a crowd and coming over for a chat; the lads with me would always wonder what made me so special that Ringy would pick me out, but it all goes back to our playing days, when I had to mark him, and let me tell you, that was some job. He was a one-off. There was nothing he couldn't do with the ball in his hand. He was as strong as he was skilful and the ultimate challenge for any back.'

Martin Óg recalled one head to head with the great man at the old Athletic Grounds in Ballintemple. 'I'd already beaten Christy to one ball, and being the sportsman that he was, he gave me a little tap on the elbow to acknowledge I'd got the better of him on that occasion. Later on in the game, the ball came in his direction, he gathered it and he tried flicking it over my head so that he could run onto it and, knowing him, probably score a goal.

'But I timed my jump well, caught the bell and drove it 80 yards back down the field. I'd no sooner cleared the ball when Ringy said to me, 'tis few lads get the better of me once, Óg, but you've done it to me twice now!' With the ball, without the ball, Ringy was the complete hurler – and it's sad he was taken from us at so young an age (58). He was the total package.'

Many scribes have often suggested that the team Martin Óg featured in ought to have won more than one All-Ireland title between 1957 and ' 63, and the final defeats to Kilkenny in both those years have never rested well with the man himself.

'That's all we won, the one in ' 59,' he opined, 'when we really should have won more than one. Circumstances and moments in games sometimes go for you and against you, but for me, we should have least won four All-Irelands between ' 57 and ' 63, and a couple of Leagues – we only won one of each.'

But there must be some solace to be drawn from the esteem that Waterford team remains held in?

'There's something in that alright. I remember, it was at Frankie Walsh's funeral, the Lord have mercy on him, we were above in Mount Sion and there was a couple of car loads of former Cork players after travelling down for it, and one of them came over to me and said that the best hurling he ever saw was the type of hurling we played between ' 57 and ' 63. He said it was fantastic hurling. And sure Babs Keating said he played hurling, after looking at the way we played, and he decided that that was the way he wanted to play his hurling.'

The morning after the '59 win, Martin Óg recalls himself and a few players bandaging up the great Larry Guinan, in the wake of some 'tired and emotional' celebrations in Portmarnock.

'Jack Furlong, Lord have mercy on him, he had a bag full of bandages and stuff for rubs and what have you. We got a bandage off Jack, some ketchup down in the (hotel) kitchen and when Guinan passed out that night, we put the ketchup on him and then bandaged him up. And when he woke up in the morning, he started asking what was after happening to him and by God, did we laugh. We weren't above the bit of fun ourselves then! We enjoyed ourselves, sure that's what you did after you put in the effort and we had a great time going around the county with the cup after that'; we were on the road for about three weeks and it was great. Great memories altogether.'

So how would Martin Óg describe his Waterford's team brand of play? 'It was fast, open hurling. There was no dilly dallying or anything like that. The ball did the work whereas the way it is now, at the present moment, the men are doing the work. I think myself, regarding next Sunday, if we play first time hurling, I think we'll beat Galway, whereas if we try and mix it with them, I don't think we will because they have 13 men starting who are six foot and over and we don't have that same level of physique. But in saying that, I reckon the biggest team I ever saw playing was the Waterford team that won the All-Ireland in '48. There were at least 13 of them six foot and over and the smallest fella on that team would have been Andy Fleming, who played with Mount Sion. Sure you had Mick Hickey from Portlaw (DK notes: I can still see Mick striding down the lane in Lahardan to greet his grandchildren off the school bus), Christy Moylan, John Keane, Eddie Carew, Kevin O'Connor, Tom Curran from Dungarvan, (John) Cusack from Clonea, Mick Hayes, sure he was well over six foot tall. They were big men, and they were great hurlers, and they'd the Celtic Cross to prove it.'

And what of the men of 2017? 'When you look at the way young (Darragh) Fives played against Cork, Cork didn't even get a shot at goal in that match. I thought he was brilliant; he hurled just like the old fashioned centre half-back; he went from one wing to the other and hurled in behind the half-back line. The centre half-back used to cover his wing half-backs, and then the wing-half backs would cover the centre half-back – they were the original sweepers so what's been done now isn't new at all.'

Martin Óg continued: 'Tadhg de Búrca is a very good hurler, Conor Gleeson is an excellent player and he's a big loss for Sunday, and our own fella, Austin (Gleeson) is a very good hurler too. He might get a bit fiery sometimes but I feel he's going to have to curb that. For me, the best place for him to play is around centre-field. He's not a man marker, so I wouldn't play him at centre-back but he's a good hurler, without a doubt in the world, and I'd be inclined to leave him out around the middle of the field where he can move around. And sure that goal against Cork was fantastic, and it's the second brilliant goal he got against Cork, he got a beauty up in Thurles a few years ago when he played wing half-forward.'

As for Sunday? 'We're going to have to be on it from when the first whistle is blown and until the last whistle is blown. But I really do expect us to be coming home next Monday with the MacCarthy Cup. I think what's in place, in addition to what we have coming on from the line is good enough to win on Sunday.'

Let's hope the legendary Martin Óg's prediction comes to pass, and that he'll have new All-Ireland champions to welcome home to Waterford next Monday night.

MORE
GREAT
SPORTS BOOKS
FROM
HERO BOOKS

 **HERO**BOOKS

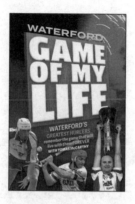

WATERFORD
GAME OF MY LIFE

25 of the greatest Waterford hurlers over the last 60 years remember the one game in their careers that defined their sporting lives.

Including: Tom Cunningham, Martin Óg Morrissey, Michael O'Connor, Larry Guinan, Jim Greene, Brian Greene, Patricia Jackman, Mossie Walsh, John Galvin, Shane Ahearne, Stephen Frampton, Fergal Hartley, Sean Cullinane, Brian Flannery, Eoin Murphy, John Mullane, Beth Carton , Paul Flynn , Dan Shanahan and Maurice Shanahan

A game that will live with each person forever.

Author: Tómas McCarthy
Print Price: €20.00
Ebook: €9.99
ISBN: 9781910827406

Buy on **Amazon**
(and paperback available in all good bookstores)

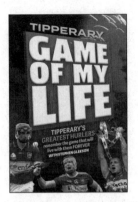

TIPPERARY
GAME OF MY LIFE

THE GREATEST TIPPERARY hurlers over the last 50 years remember the one game in blue and gold that defined their lives...

Jimmy Finn, Theo English, Tony Wall, Tadhg O'Connor, Dinny Ryan, Babs Keating, John Sheedy, Ken Hogan, Colm Bonnar, Cormac Bonnar, Declan Carr, Michael Cleary, Pat Fox, Conal Bonnar, Declan Ryan, Michael Ryan, Joe Hayes, Eamonn Corcoran, Tommy Dunne, Shane McGrath, James Woodlock, Brendan Cummins, Eoin Kelly, Michael Cahill, Brendan Maher, James Barry, Seamus Callinan and more...

A game that will live with each man forever.

Author: Stephen Gleeson
Print Price: €20.00
Ebook: €9.99
ISBN: 9781910827185

Buy on **Amazon**
(and paperback available in all good bookstores)

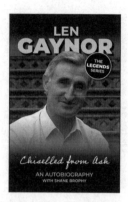

Chiselled from Ash
Len Gaynor: An Autobiography

CHISELLED FROM ASH is a story of love and honour.

It's the story of Len Gaynor's great love for the game of hurling, and how he has honoured the great game his whole life.

Len Gaynor won it all with Tipperary, finishing his career with three All-Ireland hurling titles, four Munster titles and two National League titles in the 1960s and 70s. But the flamboyant wing back also wanted to give back at the end of his career.

The Kilruane MacDonaghs clubman - and winner of three county titles - quickly proved himself to be one of the smartest and most ambitious coaches in the game.

At club level he strived to teach and help the next generation, and led his own Kilruane and neighbouring clubs to success – and at county level through the 1990s Len Gaynor managed Tipperary and Clare on the biggest stages in the game.

Chiselled from Ash is the story of one man's great love for a great game that has remained undimmed over seven decades.

Authors: Len Gaynor with Shane Brophy
Print Price: €20.00
Ebook: €9.99
ISBN: 9781910827208

Buy on **Amazon**
(and paperback available in all good bookstores)

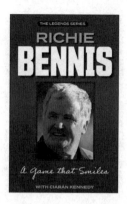

'A Game that Smiles'
The Richie Bennis Autobiography

RICHIE BENNIS IS one of the true legends remaining in the game of hurling. A towering figure in Limerick GAA, he played a central role as the county won the All-Ireland title in 1973 and then he strived as hard as anyone to see the Liam MacCarthy Cup return to the Treaty County.

It was a wait of 45 years – during which time Bennis worked at grassroots hurling in the famed Patrickswell club, where he hurled into his 40s and won 10 county titles. He also led Limerick as team manager to the 2007 All-Ireland final where they lost to Kilkenny.

In 2018, Limerick were crowned All-Ireland champions.

For Richie Bennis, a long agonising wait ended. His story is one of triumph, and heartache and personal tragedy, and a courage that was never dimmed.

Authors: Richie Bennis with Ciarán Kennedy
Print Price: €20.00
Ebook: €9.99
ISBN: 9781910827093

Buy on **Amazon**
(and paperback available in all good bookstores)

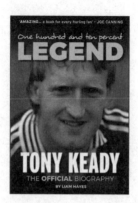

One Hundred and Ten Percent Legend
Tony Keady: The Official Biography

WHEN TONY KEADY died suddenly in August of 2017, at just 53 years of age, a whole county mourned and the rest of the country stopped in its tracks to say goodbye to a legend of the game of hurling.

Except Tony Keady was more than a legend.

In 1988, after leading Galway to a second All-Ireland title in succession, he was crowned the greatest hurler in Ireland. He was 25 years of age and there was nobody like him, nobody to touch him in the maroon No.6 shirt.

But, four years later, and still not 30, after being wrongly banned for 12 months by the GAA, he was also discarded by his own county and refused a maroon jersey the very last time he walked out onto Croke Park behind the Galway team.

A few months before his death, Tony Keady visited Liam Hayes and told him he wished to tell his own story. He felt it was time, but tragically time was not on Tony's side. One month after he died, Galway won the All-Ireland title for the first time since 1988 and 80,000 people rose from their seats in the sixth minute of the game to applaud and remember a man who was more than a legend

Tony's wife, Margaret and his daughter, Shannon and his three boys, Anthony, Harry and Jake, decided to finish telling the story of a father and a hurler who always asked those around him for '110%.

Author: Liam Hayes
Price: €20.00
Ebook: €9.99
ISBN: 9781910827048

Buy on **Amazon**
(and paperback available in all good bookstores)

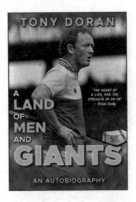

A Land of Men and Giants
The Tony Doran Autobiography

WEXFORD'S ALL-IRELAND winning hero Tony Doran was a giant in the game of hurling through the 1960s, 70s and 80s, at a time when full-forwards were ordered to plunder goals.

In his 19 years and 187 appearances as a Wexford hurler, Tony Doran successfully went for goal 131 times.

But Doran also played against giants from Kilkenny, Tipperary and Cork, and so many other counties, at a time when the game of hurling tested the wits and the courage of every man on the field.

Some of these men became giants.

A Land of Men and Giants is the story told by Tony Doran of a life spent living and competing against legendary men and true giants of the game.

A Land of Men and Giants: The Autobiography of Tony Doran is edited by award-winning writer and author Liam Hayes.

Authors: Tony Doran with Liam Hayes
Print Price: €20.00
Ebook: €9.99
ISBN: 9781910827031

Buy on **Amazon**
(and paperback available in all good bookstores)

GALWAY
GAME OF MY LIFE

TWENTY-FIVE OF Galway's greatest hurlers remember the one game that will live with them forever ...

including Jimmy Hegarty, Ned Dervan, Andy Fenton, Iggy Clarke, Sean Silke, Joe Connolly, PJ Molloy, Noel Lane, John Connolly, Mike Conneely, Anthony Cunningham, Pete Finnerty, Eanna Ryan, Gerry McInerney, John Commins, Michael Coleman, Micheál Donoghue, Padraig Kelly, Kevin Broderick, Ger Farragher, David Collins, Ollie Canning, Alan Kerins, Fergal Moore and Gearoid McInerney

... the day that defined their lives.

Author: Ollie Turner
Print Price: €20.00
Ebook: €9.99
ISBN: 9781910827284

Buy on **Amazon**
(and paperback available in all good bookstores)

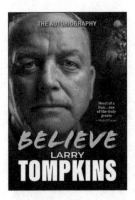

BELIEVE

Larry Tompkins: An Autobiography

HIS SELF-BELIEF WAS unbreakable.

His iron will inspirational.

Nothing could stop Larry Tompkins. No man, no team, as he made his football life the greatest story ever told in the long and brilliant history of the GAA.

Six years with his native Kildare left him empty-handed and heartbroken. He emigrated to New York to find a job and find a team he could lead to championship glory. In the United States, Tompkins' belief in himself never dimmed. He led Donegal to four New York championships in the Big Apple. He also found a new home for himself in Ireland and led Castlehaven to two Cork and Munster titles. In between, he also became the most valuable and feared footballer in Ireland.

BELIEVE is the story of a man who defied all the odds. In Cork's magnificent red shirt, he led his adopted county to two All-Ireland titles in 1989 and 90, one National League and six Munster titles, and he also was honoured with three Allstar awards.

Upon his retirement, Larry Tompkins continued to lead and inspire, and make others believe too. He managed Cork for seven years, winning Munster glory again, and drove Cork to the 1999 All-Ireland final where they agonisingly came up short.

BELIEVE is a story which proves to everyone, in every sport, that anything is possible and everything is there to be won!

Authors: Larry Tompkins with Denis Hurley
Print Price: €20.00
Ebook: €9.99
ISBN: 9781910827123

Buy on **Amazon**
(and paperback available in all good bookstores)